Dynamics of
Community Planning

Dynamics of
Community Planning

by
Neil Gilbert and **Harry Specht**
School of Social Welfare
University of California, Berkeley

Ballinger Publishing Company ● Cambridge, Massachusetts
A Subsidiary of J.B. Lippincott Company

International Standard Book Number: 0-88410-362-5

Library of Congress Catalog Card Number: 77-22182

Printed in the United States of America

Library of Congress Cataloging in Publication Data

Gilbert, Neil.
  Dynamics of community planning.

    1. City planning—United States. 2. Urban renewal—United States
I. Specht, Harry, joint author. II. Title.
HT167.G53   309.2'62'0973   77-22182
ISBN 0-88410-362-5

For:

Evan
and
Jesse

Daniel
and
Eliot

Contents

List of Figures xi

List of Tables xiii

Acknowledgements xvii

Introduction xix

Part I
Setting, Framework, and Methods

Chapter 1
Setting: Community Planning in the 1960s 1

Experiences in Community Planning: From the "City Beautiful"
 to the War on Poverty 2
Laying the Groundwork for Model Cities 6
Guidelines for Implementation 10
A Shift in Emphasis: The New Federalism 16

Chapter 2
The Analytic Framework: Propositions on Planning 27

Propositions on the Action System 32
Propositions on the Interorganizational Field 36
Propositions on the Community Context 39
Conclusion 42

Chapter 3
Methods: Indicators and Measurements of
Community Planning   47

Sources of Data   48
Operational Definitions of Indicators   52
Approach to Data Analysis   60

Part II
Community Planning System

Chapter 4
The Action System   65

Characteristics of the Action System   68

Chapter 5
Patterns of Influence and the Chain of Planning Objectives   93

Patterns of Influence and Quality of CDP   94
Patterns of Influence and the Implementation Process   99
Patterns of Influence and Performance   101
Summary   104

Chapter 6
The Interorganizational Field   107

Dimensions of the Interorganizational Field   108
Interorganizational Field and the Chain of Planning Objectives   112
Summary   120

Chapter 7
The Community Context   125

Contextual Factors and the Planning Process   129
Relationships to Other Planning Objectives   133

Part III
Outcomes, Predictions, and Applications

Chapter 8
Outcomes: The Congruence of Planning Objectives   137

Planning Process and Related Outcomes   138
Planning Products and Related Outcomes   144
Implementation Process and Program Performance   150
Summary   152

Chapter 9
Planning to Plan: An Assessment of Predictions About Model
Cities Participants   159

Picking Winners: The Bases for Planning Grant Allocations   159
Selection Criteria and Program Performance   166
A Simplified Alternative   168
Manifest and Latent Functions of Selection Procedures   170

Chapter 10
Applications: Some Guidelines for Community Planning   175

Quantitative Considerations in Planning   175
Qualitative Considerations in Planning   177

Index   181

About the Authors   185

List of Figures

2-1	Planning System	28
2-2	Framework for Analysis of Community Planning	29
4-1	Action System Characteristics and Patterns of Influence	69
5-1	Functional Designation of Funds Based on Project Summaries	94
6-1	Relationships Between Interorganizational Field Variables and Planning Objectives	109
7-1	Relationships Between Contextual Factors and Planning Objectives	129

List of Tables

3-1   Relationships Between Selected Variables and Degree of Citizen Influence in the Planning Process   61

4-1   Round Funded and Patterns of Influence   67

4-2   Model Neighborhood Area Size and Patterns of Influence   69

4-3   Percent of Racial Minorities in the Model Neighborhood Area and Patterns of Influence   71

4-4   Model Neighborhood Area Conflict and Patterns of Influence   73

4-5   Political Integration of Model Neighborhood Area Leadership and Patterns of Influence   74

4-6   Patterns of Influence and Sociopolitical Environment   75

4-7   Patterns of Influence and Resident Control Over Staff   78

4-8   Patterns of Influence and Turnover of CDA Directors   80

4-9   Percent of Transition-Period Turnover by Political Integration and Patterns of Influence   81

4-10   Associations Between Process/Task Orientations in Planning Period and Planning Period Outcomes   85

4-11   Associations Between Process/Task Orientations in First Program Year and Program Year Outcomes   86

4-12   Degree of Professionalization of CDA Staff and Patterns of Influence   89

5-1   Patterns of Influence and Ratios of "Best/Worst" CDPs   97

5-2   Patterns of Influence and the Percent of Categorical Funds in the CDP   98

5-3   Patterns of Influence and Percent of Local Funds in the CDP Budget   98

5-4   Patterns of Influence and Quality of Agency Participation in Planning   99

5-5   Patterns of Influence and Number of Agencies in the CDP   100

5-6   Patterns of Influence and Implementation of Citizen Participation   100

5-7   Patterns of Influence and Implementation of Service Coordination Objectives   101

5-8   Percentages of Supplemental Funds Spent by Model Cities at Six Months and Twelve Months   103

5-9   Patterns of Influence and the Percentages of Cities with Low Rates of Spending at Six Months, Twelve Months, and Per Capita Spending at Twelve Months   104

5-10   Patterns of Influence and "Most/Least Successful" First-Year Programs   104

6-1   Associations Between Interorganizational Field Variables   108

6-2   Types of Agencies, Numbers of Cities in Which Each Type Participated, and Intensity of Participation   110

6-3   Associations Between Interorganizational Field Variables and Patterns of Influence   112

6-4   Chief Executive Commitment and Patterns of Influence   113

6-5   Patterns of Influence and Quality of Agency Participation in Planning   114

6-6   Associations Between Interorganizational Field Variables and Planning Products   115

6-7   Associations Between Interorganizational Field Variables and Plan Implementation Variables   117

6-8   Associations Between Interorganizational Field Variables and Program Performance Variables   118

6-9   Number of Agencies Involved in the Planning Process and Degree of Success in Coordination   121

7-1   Associations Between Three Contextual Factors   128

7-2   Associations Between Contextual Factors and Elements in the Planning Process   130

7-3   City Size and Patterns of Influence   130

7-4   Patterns of Influence in Small and Large Cities   130

7-5   City Size and Patterns of Influence for Cities with Different Degrees of Urban Renewal Experience   132

8-1	Associations Between Patterns of Influence in the Planning Process and Other Model Cities Objectives	142
8-2	Associations Between Measures of CDP Quality and Other Model Cities Planning Objectives	147
8-3	Associations Between Outcome Measures of Implementation Process and Program Performance	152
9-1	Associations Among PGRP Selection Criteria Ratings	166
9-2	Associations Between Planning Grant Review Project and Performance Indicators	167
9-3	Associations Between Length of Experience and Performance Indicators	169

Acknowledgements

This study of community planning efforts in Model Cities began in 1971 and extended over a period of five years.

During the course of this study our work benefited from the generous assistance of a number of friends, colleagues, and organizations. Marshall Kaplan, Gans, and Kahn (MKGK), a firm of planners in San Francisco, was helpful in providing the initial support that got us started on this study. Armin Rosencranz, a member of that firm, was a particular source of encouragement. At later stages in the research, additional support was provided by the Committee on Research at the University of California, Berkeley and the Administration on Aging, Department of Health, Education and Welfare, for which we are most grateful.

In the data collection phase of the study we received excellent cooperation from John W. McLean and David D. Johnson on the administrative staff of the Department of Housing and Urban Development. Peter Clute, of the San Francisco Office of HUD gave us exceedingly perceptive advice. The retrieval of data at HUD's Washington offices would not have been possible without the help of several people there who have an uncanny ability to keep track of information: David Pollack, Ursula Hill, Richard Koory, Bennie Lieberman, and James Beasly. The following HUD deskmen were generous enough to grant us time for interviews: Don Dodge, John Tuite, Robert Dodge, Conrad Egan, Walter Erhardt, Michael Janis, Anna Payne, Andrew Bell, Barbara Slotnik, Walter O. Anderson, and Kinsey Potter. Their thoughtful and frank responses contributed significantly to our findings. We would also like to thank the U.S. Conference of Mayors for cosponsoring the study survey of Model Cities Agencies.

Lynne Roberts, our colleague at Berkeley, helped us to organize the data for the computer analysis. Charlane Brown (who was then our student and is now our colleague) was an indefatigable research assistant, coder, analyst, and coauthor of one part of the study which is published elsewhere. Sarah Johnson, Robert Paulson, and Susan Chu, our students, also worked as coders. Riva Specht and Eliot D. Specht contributed thoughtful editorial assistance. Marcy McGaugh provided cheerul assistance in typing and retyping our drafts.

Some of the findings from this study have been published in the *Public Administration Review, Social Service Review, Sociological Review Monograph,* and *Social Work.*[a] We thank the editors of those journals for permission to incorporate portions of those articles in this book.

Finally, we owe special appreciation to the members of our families whose good spirits and friendly support were a continuous source of renewal.

Our list of acknowledgements is long. However, there were thousands of citizens, professionals, and political leaders who invested vast amounts of time, energy, and concern in the desire to realize the benefits of community planning. Our firm hope is that we, in some small way, will illuminate the meaning of their efforts.

Neil Gilbert and Harry Specht
University of California, Berkeley
May 1977

[a] Neil Gilbert and Harry Specht, "'Picking Winners': Federal Discretion and Local Experiences as Bases for Planning Grant Allocations," *Public Administration Review* 34, no. 6 (November/December 1974); Neil Gilbert, Harry Specht, and Charlane Brown, "Demographic Correlates of Citizen Participation: Race, Size, and Citizen Influence," *Social Service Review* (December 1974); Neil Gilbert and Harry Specht, "Socio-political Correlates of Community Action: An Analysis of Conflict, Political Integration, and Citizen Influence," *Sociological Review Monograph*, no. 21 (November 1975); Neil Gilbert and Harry Specht, "Process vs. Task in Social Planning," *Social Work* (May 1977).

Introduction

Model Cities was the first program organized by the Department of Housing and Urban Development (HUD), which was established in 1965, and it was the last of the Great Society efforts to encourage and strengthen systematic community planning at the local level. Revenue sharing (both "general" and "special"), the major new means by which the federal government provides resources to local communities, represents a movement away from federal concern with the dynamics and techniques by which local communities utilize their resources.[1] But Model Cities, and many of the New Frontier and Great Society programs preceding it, have made community planning in the United States a substantially different enterprise than it was twenty years ago. Despite the disappointment in the 1970s with many of the Great Society programs and despair over the possibilities of achieving their goals, social legislation continues to reflect many of the changes wrought in the preceding twenty years. For example, there is hardly a piece of federal legislation that does not require communities to find means to assure citizen participation in the planning and implementation of social programs,[2] an important legacy of the New Frontier and the Great Society. Concern with increasing the coordination among, and accountability of, social programs certainly has not diminished on the local level, and interest in evaluation of social programs continues unabated.[3] Moreover, regardless of recent changes in federal-state-local relations, social planning in urban communities can only continue to grow in importance as efforts are made to solve the increasingly complex problems of our cities. Therefore, it seems important to discover what can be learned from the Model Cities experience.

Several analyses of the Model Cities Program have already been done.[4] Although some earlier commentaries were positive,[5] the general verdict appears to be that the Model Cities Program failed.[6] Why, then, the reader should most certainly ask, do we offer yet another analysis? Is the Gilbert-Specht verdict different? Our answer to that question is neither "yes" nor "no," because in this study we do not address the success of the Model Cities Program *sui generis.* We ask an entirely different set of questions. But before we describe the questions our analysis addresses, we want to comment on the negative critiques of the Model Cities Program.

The overriding objective of the Model Cities Program, stated in the legislation creating it, was to demonstrate how the federal government could help cities to improve "the quality of urban life" and help

> cities of all sizes . . . to plan, develop, and carry out locally prepared and scheduled comprehensive city demonstration programs containing new and imaginative proposals to rebuild or revitalize large slum and blighted areas; to expand housing, job, and income opportunities; to reduce dependence on welfare payments; to improve educational facilities and programs; to combat disease and ill health; to reduce the incidence of crime and delinquency; to establish better homes and jobs; and generally to improve living conditions for the people who live in such areas, and to accomplish these objectives through the most effective and economical concentration of Federal, State, and local public and private efforts to improve the quality of urban life.[7]

Certainly, these are commendable objectives, so sweeping and far-reaching as to inspire high hopes. They are also, however, *unattainable* and *unmeasurable,* at least insofar as the financial and legal bases of the Model Cities Program were concerned. They were *unattainable* because the size and scope of the resources allocated to the program precluded its making a significant impact on something as vague and vast as "the quality of life" in 147 cities. And the objective was *unmeasurable* because even if it were assumed that the resources allocated to the Model Cities Program could have impacted significantly on "the quality of urban life," and that the changes in "the quality of urban life" could be measured, no one would know *how much* of a change would be considered a significant enough improvement in "the quality of urban life" to determine success.

On a more practical level, the Model Cities Program was supposed to demonstrate how cities could bring about a redistribution of resources so as to benefit the poor and how the federal categorical system of program grants to cities could be reformed. (We will discuss some of the historical bases of these objectives in more detail in the first chapter.) Thinking about the Model Cities Program objectives at this more practical level, we believe that a critique of the program as "successful" or "unsuccessful" is misguided. Specifically, it is wishful thinking to expect to eliminate poverty and to reform the federal categorical system by awarding fairly modest planning grants to 147 cities with the promise that *if* they did their work well they would be given relatively modest supplementary grants and that they *might* be given special consideration in competing with other cities for federal categorical grants.[8] To critique the Model Cities Program from that perspective, it seems to us, is to preordain a negative verdict. Only 147 cities received these modest allocations of funds; and even within these 147 cities, the benefits of the program were directed at relatively small sections of the cities (10 percent of the population, or populations of 15,000, whichever was larger). Thus, a city was not only competing with hundreds of other cities for the planning and supplemental grants that would accrue if it became a Model City, but *within* each Model City the allocation of special resources to the Model Neighborhoods heightened the competition for resources among various neighborhoods and groups. The task of the Model Cities was made even more formidable when we add that in order to plan successfully for the Model Neighborhoods, the cities had to deal with the panoply of city, state, regional, and federal agencies that have varying degrees of responsibility for hundreds of federal programs, programs that apply to varying jurisdictional boundaries, that operate under different rules and regulations, and that have different application and funding procedures and different reporting systems.

Even though there would seem little likelihood of achieving the objectives of redistribution and reform of the federal categorical system under these conditions, the verdict is not entirely negative. For example, although Frieden and Kaplan (who have analyzed the Model Cities Program from the perspective of achievement of these major objectives) report that overall the program fell short of the mark, they also indicate that there were some successes. They say that Model Cities

loosened the federal strings on grants-in-aid . . . showed the way toward a style of federal administration and review that could reconcile local flexibility with national purposes . . . [and] confirmed that further attention is needed to bolster the mayor's political ability to help the poor, improve the capacity of local governments to manage complex programs, and to strengthen mayoral control over federal resources going into their cities.[9]

The Model Cities Program was conceived as a *demonstration* program. As with many large-scale demonstration programs that attempt to experiment, and to find ways to deal, with social problems, the demonstration objectives of the Model Cities Program were forgotten almost before the legislation that established the program had been approved by Congress and the president. This is not surprising in light of the many political and organizational conflicts that had to be resolved even before the program was announced, not to mention the complex problems of implementation.

As stated earlier, our study does not approach the Model Cities Program from the viewpoint of its effects on the larger societal problems of redistribution of resources among income groups and the reform of federal-local funding relationships. Rather, we focus on questions about *how* the Model Cities engaged in the planning and implementation of their programs. We have no *absolute* measures of success of the Model Cities Program,—nor does anyone else. However, there were *relative* degrees of success among the Model Cities in the ways they planned their programs, in the degree of citizen influence in planning, in the number of agencies participating in planning and the quality of that participation, and in the amounts of allocated money the cities were able to spend on the programs that they planned. Using these measures, as well as a number of other demographic, organizational, and process measures, we have analyzed how communities responded to the opportunities of the Model Cities Program.

Our effort is devoted to an assessment of what Model Cities demonstrated about social planning at the local level. The program, as a national demonstration, provided a unique opportunity to test some theoretical propositions and professional beliefs about social planning. From the perspective of social scientists and practitioners interested in the subject of social planning, it is certainly unusual to have the chance to study 147 cities working within approximately the same time frame, under the same legislative mandate and program guidelines, and with approximately the same resources, to achieve the same objectives. Many studies of community planning deal with a single case; very few deal with more than ten to twenty cities; and most studies of community behavior that deal with numbers large enough to allow for comparisons between categories of cities use census data or survey questionnaires based on responses to hypothetical problems and situations. Because of the nature of the Model Cities Program and the kinds of data available (chapter 3), this analysis deals with the responses of a large population of cities over a two-year period as perceived by program officials at various levels.

This book is organized in three parts. Part I is introductory and contains three chapters. Chapter 1 describes the history of community planning in the 1960s and the organization of the Model Cities Program. Chapter 2 is a discussion of the analytic framework used in the study, and chapter 3 describes our methodological approach.

Part II examines the major elements in three levels of community planning: the "action system" (chapters 4 and 5); the "interorganizational field" (chapter 6); and the "community context" (chapter 7). The analyses are focused upon how different elements relate to each other and to program outcomes.

In Part III we analyze the congruence of program objectives, efforts to predict outcomes, and the practice implications of our findings. Chapter 8 is a discussion of how the desired program outcomes were linked in a "chain of planning objectives." And in chapter 9 we analyze and assess the utility of methods used by federal planners to judge the potential of Model Cities program applicants. Our conclusions about community planning are discussed in the final chapter.

NOTES

1. For example, see The State and Local Assistance Act of 1972 (Public Law 95-512 86 *Stat* 919); Harvey Perloff and Richard Nathan, eds., *Revenue Sharing in the City* (Baltimore: The Johns Hopkins Press, 1968); Selma J. Muskin and John F. Cotton, *Sharing Federal Funds for State and Local Needs* (New York: Praeger Publishers, 1969); Melvin Mogulof, "Elements of a Special-Revenue-Sharing Proposal for the Social Services: Goal Setting, Decentralization, Planning and Education," *Social Service Review* 47, no. 1 (March 1973): 593-604; Edward C. Banfield, "Revenue Sharing in Theory and Practice," *The Public Interest* 23 (Spring 1971): 36-49; Martha N. Ozawa, "Revenue Sharing and Its Implications for Social Welfare Programs," *Child Welfare* 51 (March 1972): 140-51; Michael D. Raegan, *The New Federalism* (New York: Oxford University Press, 1972); Paul Terrell "Citizen Participation and General Revenue Sharing," *Social Work* 20, no. 6 (November 1975): 429-35.

2. For example: *The Comprehensive Employment and Training Act of 1973* (P.L. 93-203) requires that sponsors submit program plans which, among other things, assure participation of community-based groups in developing the plan; the 1973 legislation extending the authorization of the Law Enforcement Assistance Administration through 1976 (P.L. 93-138) requires that all planning

meetings be open to the public when final action is taken on state plans and that there be participation in the planning process by citizens and community groups; *The Comprehensive Older Americans Services Amendments of 1973* (P.L. 93-29) requires that Area Agencies on Aging take into account the views of recipients of services and establish advisory councils consisting of representatives of the target population and the general public; *Title XX of the 1974 Amendments to the Social Security Act* (P.L. 93-647) establishes a federal requirement that states publish their social services plans in advance of implementation and accept public comment for a forty-five-day period. Amendments to the plan must also be published in advance, and comment accepted for thirty days. During the periods of comment, concerned individuals and organizations are to have the opportunity to study and evaluate the plans and to let appropriate officials know whether they believe the plans meet their community's needs for social services; *The Child and Family Services Act of 1975* (S. 626; H.R. 2966; not yet enacted) requires that sponsors of programs, whether units of government or voluntary agencies, set up a Child and Family Service Council, half of which must be composed of parents selected by other parents of children served by the program and half of which must be economically disadvantaged; under *The National Planning and Resources Development Act of 1974* (P.L. 93-641), state agencies created to implement the program must create and be advised by statewide Health Coordinating Councils, at least half of the members of which must be consumers.

3. The following are selected examples of the vast literature that can be cited to support this point: Peter H. Rossi and Walter Williams, eds., *Evaluating Social Programs: Theory, Practice, and Politics* (New York: Seminar Press, 1972); Carol H. Weiss, ed., *Evaluating Action Programs: Readings in Social Action and Education* (Boston: Allyn and Bacon, 1972); Tony Tripodi, Phillip Fellin, and Irwin Epstein, *Social Program Evaluation* (Itasca, Ill.: F.E. Peacock, Inc., 1971); Edwin J. Thomas, Claude L. Walter, and Kevin O'Flaherty, "Computer-Assisted Assessment and Modification: Possibilities and Illustrative Data," *Social Service Review* 48 (June 1974): 170-83; William C. Sze and June G. Hopps, eds., *Evaluation and Accountability in Human Services* (Cambridge, Mass.: Schenkman Publishers Co., 1974); Edward Newman and Jerry Turem, "The Crisis of Accountability," *Social Work* 19, no. 1 (January 1974); 5-17; Eleanor C. Bennet and Marvin Weisinger, *Program Evaluation, A Resource Handbook for Vocational Rehabilitation* (New York: ICD Rehabilitation and Research Center, 1974); R.O. Washington, *Program Evaluation in the Human Services* (Milwaukee: Center for Advanced Studies in Human Services, University of Wisconsin, n.d., circa 1973).

4. Bernard J. Frieden and Marshall Kaplan, *The Politics of Neglect: Urban Aid from Model Cities to Revenue Sharing* (Cambridge, Mass.: MIT Press, 1975); Christopher C. Demuth, "Deregulating the Cities," *The Public Interest* 44 (Summer 1976): 115-28; Charles M. Haar, *Between the Idea and the Reality: A Study in the Origin, Fate and Legacy of the Model Cities Program* (Boston: Little, Brown and Co., 1975); Roland L. Warren, "Model Cities First Round: Politics, Planning, and Participation," *Journal of the American Institute of Planners* 35, no. 4 (July 1969): 245-52; Roland L. Warren, "The Model Cities Program: An Assessment," *Social Welfare Forum, 1971* (New York: Columbia

University Press, 1971), pp. 151-64; Roland L. Warren, Stephen M. Rose, and Ann F. Bergunder, *The Structure of Urban Reform* (Lexington, Mass.: D.C. Heath and Co., 1974); Department of Housing and Urban Development, *The Model Cities Program: A Comparative Analysis of the Planning Process in Eleven Cities* (Washington, D.C.: Government Printing Office, 1970); Department of Housing and Urban Development, *Ten Model Cities—A Comparative Analysis of the Second Round Planning Year* (Washington, D.C.: Government Printing Office, 1974); Neil Gilbert and Harry Specht, *The Model Cities Program, A Comparative Analysis of Participating Cities: Process, Product, Performance, and Prediction* (Washington, D.C.: Government Printing Office, 1973); Fred Jordan, "Model Cities in Perspective: A Selective History," in *Model Cities: A Report on Progress*, special issue of Model Cities Service Center Bulletin (Washington, D.C.: Government Printing Office, 1971); U.S. President's Task Force on Model Cities, *Report, Model Cities: A Step Towards the New Federalism* (Washington, D.C.: Government Printing Office, 1970) ("Banfield Report"); James L. Sundquist and David W. Davis, *Making Federalism Work* (Washington, D.C.: Brookings Institution, 1969).

5. For example, see U.S. President's Task Force on Model Cities; Sundquist and Davis.

6. For example, see Frieden and Kaplan; Haar; and Warren.

7. *Demonstration Cities and Metropolitan Development Act of 1966* (P.L. 89-754).

8. Frieden and Kaplan point out that between 1967 and 1973 Congress allocated an average of approximately $335 million per year total for the entire Model Cities Program, a sum that could hardly be expected to make an impact on the "quality of life" in 147 cities, especially when the target populations were composed of large proportions of people living in poverty (p. 271). They also note that specific awards of categorical funds for model neighborhoods through a special system of "earmarking" in the federal departments "remained elusive" (p. 107).

9. Ibid., p. 248.

✻ **Part I**

Setting, Framework, and Methods

❋ **Chapter 1**

Setting: Community Planning in the 1960s

The shape of community planning was transformed in the 1960s with strong financial and legislative support from the federal government. Three major factors contributed to this transformation. First, the citizen participation movement, with its roots in civil-rights efforts, and the Economic Opportunity Program of 1964 required that decision making for community planning be carried (and sometimes dragged) from the backrooms of political clubs and the executive chambers of blue-ribbon panels to the broader community, with more diverse actors playing roles of "community spokesmen."

The second factor contributing to the transformation of community planning was the expansion of human services programs. Up until the 1960s the traditional focus of public planning had been on physical development. In the 1960s social welfare planning, previously relegated to the private/voluntary planning efforts of local health and welfare councils, became an important concern of government.

The third factor was the strong desire of government, particularly at the federal level, to achieve higher degrees of coordination of national grant-in-aid programs at the local level.

This transformation of community planning occurred in response to a number of concerns that marked federally initiated attempts to improve community well-being, which culminated in the Model Cities Program in 1966. Of the many policies and programs that contributed to this development, the Urban Renewal program and the Economic Opportunity program were foremost. Experience gained in these programs, both the setbacks and achievements, influenced 'the thinking of those who created the Model Cities Program. We will briefly sketch some salient features of the urban renewal and antipoverty efforts. Our objective is to underscore how the design of the Model Cities Program was intended to overcome and resolve the obstacles and dilemmas encountered in earlier community planning experiences.

EXPERIENCES IN COMMUNITY PLANNING: FROM THE "CITY BEAUTIFUL" TO THE WAR ON POVERTY

Community planning in the United States has its roots in city planning. Beginning as a social reform movement in the latter part of the nineteenth century, it was concerned largely with land-use control and keeping urban development free of politics. The spirit of the movement was essentially rationalistic and utopian; the thrust was toward good government that would utilize science and expertise to design the City Beautiful.[1] Physical planning became an integral part of urban development; by 1964 over 90 percent of cities with a population in excess of 10,000 had a public planning agency.[2]

In the 1920s, efforts of the Regional Planning Association of America to introduce proposals and experiments to combine physical and social planning were backed by men such as Lewis Mumford and Clarence Stein. These efforts, however, did not alter the overriding concern of planning with physical development.[3] The major support for economic and social planning in the United States developed later during the New Deal administration, World War II, and the Kennedy and Johnson administrations. As the realm of public responsibility for planning extended from city design, to economic programs, to social and ecological concerns, so did the parameters of planning enlarge to include a wide range of disciplines and interests to deal with a variety of institutional concerns.

Contemporary community planning is significantly different from earlier efforts because of the strong role played by the federal government. Contemporary community planning, a post-World War II phenomenon, began with the federal government's support of local urban renewal programs. These programs were put forth in the Housing Act of 1949, legislation planned with ambitious hope of producing "a decent home and suitable living environment for every American family, thus contributing to the development and redevelopment of communities and to the advancement of the growth, wealth, and security of the nation." Measured against these objectives, the program's performance was recounted in the rather bleak statistics of displacement of the urban slum-dweller in favor of high-rental housing and commercial enterprises. As depicted by one widely quoted and highly critical analysis of the program, the slum-dweller was uprooted and dislocated by the merciless force of the "federal bulldozer."[4] Despite this criticism, urban renewal was not without redeeming features. A balanced account of the program's performance must include its positive impact on civic improvements, such as providing incentives for public school construction by crediting their costs to the city's share of local matching funds and creating the economic possibility of developing inner-city cultural centers such as Lincoln Center of the Performing Arts in New York City. In addition, urban renewal projects helped cities to rebuild downtown areas, thereby inducing industries to remain in the city, thus increasing the tax base for city revenues. The case can be made that some of these benefits did "trickle down" to the economically disadvantaged. But the cost was dear.[5]

Generally speaking, it might be said that where they worked best, renewal programs often were a financial success for cities and a social failure for the poor. The price of rejuvenated downtowns, new luxury high-rise apartments, and increased tax revenues was charged largely against the disadvantaged populations of the cities. In urban renewal the hopes of "a decent home and suitable living environment for every American family" were twisted by the pressing realities of land values, construction costs, and the strength of the profit motive to turn public purpose to private gain. In addition, there were myriad inner-city social problems that physical development uncovered and often exacerbated, but usually failed to solve.

Critical analyses point not only to the hardships suffered by slum neighborhood residents but also to the processes that brought about these hardships. Specifically, the problem was that the people most affected by renewal activities had little influence on the planning processes by which the future of neighborhoods was determined. Not that the program denied citizen participation. On the contrary, the requirement for citizen participation was a significant ingredient of the Seven Point Workable Program in the 1954 amendments to the Housing Act of 1949. However, the *particular* citizens that participated and the *means* by which they were selected were left open to various interpretations. The most common outcome was that the mayor or city council appointed a citywide citizen's advisory committee composed of civic leaders representing various groups and interests in the community. These blue-ribbon panels served mostly the symbolic function of endorsing renewal activities as the legitimate "public interest." But representation of low-income neighborhood residents, those most directly affected by renewal activities, was neither mandatory nor common.

As renewal programs grew, and experience with neighborhood-based opposition increased, greater consideration was given to citizen participation at the neighborhood level. On the whole, though, local citizen participation did not play a strong role in renewal planning. After a detailed account of citizen participation in an urban renewal program, Rossi and Dentler conclude:

> If we take the Hyde Park-Kenwood Community Conference as repre-senting the upper limits of effectiveness attainable by citizen participation ... then we must conclude that the maximum role to be played by a citizen participation movement in urban renewal is primarily a passive one.[6]

Similarly, Scott Greer quotes a renewal official who stated: "By and large, people don't understand what we're after—or even what we're talking about. This is fortunate, for if they did, we'd all have to run for cover."[7]

In contrast to urban renewal, the Economic Opportunity Act of 1964 stressed social programming and active participation of local residents in planning and implementation of what came to be known as the "war on poverty" or "the antipoverty program." The "maxi-mum feasible participation" clause of the Economic Opportunity Act of 1964, which received scant attention during legislative hear-ings, gave rise to a stormy history of citizen participation, the success and failures of which have been chronicled in the popular media and in community planning literature.[8]

Of course, the antipoverty agenda contained other objectives, and it would be remiss to ignore the many useful and needed services it provided such as health care, day care, legal aid, family planning, and education. However, the involvement of local residents in planning services and allocating resources for their communities was seen by many as the major innovative device for social reform in the anti-poverty program. Citizen participation was perceived as a major in-strument for institutional change.

At the extreme, citizen participation was interpreted as commu-nity control over program resources by locally elected boards of resident representatives. This interpretation challenged the power and authority of established political structures, social welfare agen-cies, and traditional community planning organizations. And as would be expected, where attempts were made to carry decentraliza-tion to the neighborhood level, bitter conflicts frequently ensued.

For example, at the annual meeting of the United States Conference of Mayors in 1965, there was vigorous debate on a resolution to propose an amendment to the Economic Opportunity Act that would give local governments greater control over the program. Although that resolution was not adopted, the debate brought to light the uncomfortable reality that many local antipoverty groups were wrestling for political power with popularly elected (and sometimes Democratic) big city mayors. Citizen participation in the antipoverty program underscored a continuing dilemma of community planning, one that is likely to continue as greater responsibility for deciding on the allocation of federal funds is shifted to local officials through schemes for general and special revenue sharing: how to create viable community planning structures that share power and decision-making authority among contending interests while maintaining the functional integrity of locally elected officials.

The coordination of local services, a traditional area of concern to community planners, gained special prominence in the antipoverty program. One reason that coordinating activities were accentuated in the mid-1960s had to do with the tremendous expansion of federal grant-in-aid programs. Between 1962 and 1966 it is estimated that the number of federal categorical grant programs increased from 160 to 349; by 1971 there were over 500 of these programs.[9] So many local private, quasi-public, and public organizations received various federal grants, that mayors of large cities found it difficult just to keep abreast of the amounts, sources, and purposes of these grants.

The coordination of a city's social welfare related activities involves not only large numbers and different types of organizations, but also crossing of the jurisdictional lines of various public bodies. For example, a city might get services from a county public health department, a state department of public assistance, a state agency for unemployment compensation, and a local board of education that is either elected or appointed and that has its own taxing power. One of the reasons that many antipoverty agencies were established as private nonprofit corporations rather than as units of city government was that attempts to coordinate interjurisdictional public bodies by a city agency was thought to be more likely to encounter stiff resistance.[10]

On the whole, though, the disengagement of antipoverty agencies from city hall did not enhance coordination. In many cases, struggles erupted between city hall and antipoverty agencies which diminished the capacity of both sides to coordinate services. As available evidence suggests, coordination in the antipoverty program achieved limited results.[11]

This brief sketch of the urban renewal and antipoverty programs does not express the complex sum of successes and failures that accompanied these efforts, if indeed such a sum is calculable. The major purpose of this discussion is to highlight some of the experiences that set the stage for one of the most substantial ventures in community planning ever initiated by the federal government, an effort that President Johnson promised would "combine physical reconstruction and rehabilitation with effective social programs throughout the rebuilding process" and "link our concern for the total welfare of the person with our desire to improve the physical city in which he lives."[12] This venture in community planning was framed in the enabling legislation of the *Demonstration Cities and Metropolitan Development Act of 1966* (P.L. 89-754) which was implemented through what has become known as the Model Cities Program.

The lessons of urban renewal and the antipoverty program as well as other previous efforts at urban improvement were useful to planners of the Model Cities Program, even where results were considerably less or different than anticipated. As Fred Jordan observes:

> That those lessons were, more frequently than not, instructive of what *not* to do rather than what to do did not lessen their value for the group of men and women who were planning the program, working for passage of enabling legislation, and, thereafter, erecting the policy framework that would give it life and substance.[13]

LAYING THE GROUNDWORK FOR MODEL CITIES

The idea for the Model Cities Program was initially proposed to President Johnson in the summer of 1965 by Walter Reuther, president of AFL-CIO Industrial Union Department, and Mayor Jerome Cavanaugh of Detroit.[14] Reuther's plan was for a concentrated renewal effort that would focus upon two cities (one of which would be Detroit) and deliver a coordinated package of federal grant-in-aid programs for community development. Detroit had had some successful experiences with a model neighborhood type program and Mayor Cavanaugh was enthusiastic about expanding the effort. Shortly after receiving this proposal, President Johnson appointed a Task Force on Urban Problems headed by Robert C. Wood, an MIT professor of political science, who was later to become undersecretary and then secretary of HUD. The Wood Task Force included Reuther and Cavanaugh, as well as Senator Abraham Ribicoff, Charles Haar, William Rafsky, Whitney Young, Jr., Ben Heineman, and Edgar Kaiser. The members of the Task Force on Urban Problems were selected, according to James, "with an eye to avoiding people committed to existing programs."[15] The charge given this task force was virtually as broad as its title: to develop innovative programs that would address what was coming to be called "the urban crisis." Wood recalled later that, as they deliberated in the aftermath of the Watts riot, the task force wanted to avoid the crash mobilization approach to program development engendered by the crisis atmosphere. "We wanted a program that would be coordinated . . . and that would produce a changed environment."[16]

In January of 1966 the task force's proposal for the Demonstration Cities program was announced. As envisioned in the proposal, the program was to be a comprehensive effort to blend social and physical planning and to concentrate federal and local resources on selected target neighborhoods in a number of cities. The program that the task force had in mind was originally thought of as a "demonstration," an experiment that would show what could be done by massive concentration of resources in six or eight cities. Political considerations, however, required that the size of the program be increased so that it would yield enough slices to at least whet the congressional appetite, about one to every state and a few extra "to small cities such as those likely to produce chairmen of Congressional committees and subcommittees."[17] Thus, the task force proposed a program to involve sixty-six cities; by the time Congress finished legislating, the final number had reached 150 cities.

While the rhetoric that invariably accompanies the creation of new programs promised a major effort and grand achievements on the order of nothing less than rebirth of American cities, this program, as its name implied, was destined to be large enough only to *demonstrate* what a major effort *might* achieve. As HUD Secretary Robert Weaver explained, the program was to be a demonstration for the benefit of all cities of the "total attack" approach to urban problems.[18]

The task force proposal contained certain key elements gleaned from previous experiences in community development. The incorporation of citizen participation in the design of the Model Cities Program was considered desirable, yet the task force realized that mayors would find this program element acceptable only in a moderate form. The mayors had developed great sensitivity to any program that might engage them in a replay of the antipoverty struggles. Hence, the Demonstration Cities proposal sought more to improve upon the citizen participation model of urban renewal than to repeat the patterns of the antipoverty program. As Jordan observes:

The phrase which dominated the early developmental phases of Model Cities work within HUD was "planning with, not for, people." That was one place where Urban Renewal had stubbed its toe. What HUD was attempting to do with citizen participation was avoid repetition of the Urban Renewal mistake. It was not seeking to pick up from OEO the ball of community action and confrontation.[19]

Mayoral support was required not only to push for congressional approval of the proposed program, but also to achieve one of the major program objectives: coordination of local agencies. Thus, while citizen participation was down-played, the role of city chief executives was elevated by placing the program under the authority of the mayor's office. In addition, the task force decided that a period of comprehensive physical and social planning should precede the action phase of the Model Cities Program. The emphasis on local planning in the Model Cities Program was partly a response to the lack of planning that had taken place in local antipoverty programs, where intentions to plan were sacrificed in the hurry to implement, and partly a device to facilitate program coordination.[20]

The Demonstration Cities proposal reached Congress at an inauspicious moment for a major new urban development bill. The long-time head of the House Subcommittee on Housing and Urban Affairs, Albert Rains, had just retired and had been replaced by a less powerful and less experienced chairman. The chairman of the corresponding Senate subcommittee, Senator John Sparkman, was unenthusiastic about introducing a new piece of major urban legislation a year after Congress had passed a housing bill that included a controversial rent supplement program. Moreover, the Department of Housing and Urban Development (HUD) was barely one year old, and the HUD officials responsible for guiding the bill through Congress were relatively inexperienced in legislative maneuvering. In sum, the congressional voyage of the Demonstration Cities Act was a stormy one.[21]

Congressional hearings on the Demonstration Cities bill began in early March, 1966, at which time the mayors of the big cities expressed considerable ambivalence about the plan. While interested in obtaining additional federal funds to cope with urban problems, they were concerned about the extent to which Demonstration Cities might become an allocative device that would borrow from Peter to pay Paul. Generally, the mayors feared that federal funds for urban renewal would be diverted to the Demonstration Cities, leaving the cities not selected with nothing. This concern was reinforced by the small number of cities (sixty-six) proposed for the program. Specifically, the mayors were dissatisfied with the proposed levels of funding and objected to the idea of selecting program participants by means of a planning competition. As Mayor Lindsay of New York put it: "A Competition among America's cities, with the fate of the poor at stake, is not a very attractive prospect for local officials."[22]

Of the various complaints expressed by mayors about different features of the bill, surprisingly few questions were raised about the element of citizen participation. On the whole, the issues of citizen participation, which were to dominate the early history of the Model Cities Program in many localities, attracted little attention during congressional hearings. Those who drafted the bill clearly intended the statutory formula of "widespread citizen participation" to imply a milder version of citizen involvement than the "maximum feasible participation" mandated by the Economic Opportunity Act of 1964. Secretary Weaver in his House testimony did not place much emphasis on citizen participation, mentioning only that the type of participation might vary from city to city.[23] This general response to the citizen participation component of the Model Cities Program forms an interesting parallel to the reception given to the "maximum feasible participation" clause during the hearings on antipoverty legislation. While in retrospect the phrase "maximum feasible participation" is seen to contain politically explosive possibilities, at the time of the Economic Opportunity Act hearings this phrase seemed just as innocuous as the "widespread citizen participation" of the Demonstration Cities bill, and received as little attention.[24]

However, there were some congressional reservations. The administration's initial request for funding in the amount of $2.3 billion over five years seemed a very costly and lengthy commitment for an experimental program that would impact on a few cities. Moreover, a number of southern Democrats and some Republicans balked at the bill's requirement that in selecting program participants HUD "give maximum consideration" to whether a proposed demonstration plan would "counteract the segregation of housing by race or income."[25] With these reservations on Capitol Hill and mayoral support still running lukewarm, administration officials met in early June to assess the bill's chances and to determine whether enough political muscle could be exerted to push it through Congress. At this meeting, support for the bill was on the wane when Lawrence O'Brien, the postmaster general, made a fiery speech admonishing his colleagues not to quit on one of the president's major proposals. Those present at the meeting, later credited the decision to support the bill to O'Brien's persuasive appeal.[26]

A number of alterations were required to make the bill more palatable to the mayors and to defuse congressional opposition:

extra funds for urban renewal projects in demonstration cities were authorized; the housing desegregation provision was reduced to a few innocent words about "maximizing opportunities in the choice of housing accomodations for all citizens;" HUD was prohibited from requiring school busing as a condition for participation; funding of supplemental grants was authorized for a period of two years in the amount of $900 million;[27] and an additional $12 million was authorized for a second planning year in fiscal 1968, increasing the number of cities that could participate to approximately 150, at least in the program's planning stage, which considerably broadened the program's potential base of support. Of these various changes in the bill, the decision to double the size of the program by expanding it to cover about 150 cities probably had the most significant consequences. This increase, James notes,

> represented a substantial dilution of the focus and intensity of the Model Cities experiment. Necessary as it might have been to gain crucial legislative support, it increased the supervisory task of the Model Cities Administration (MCA) without correcting the imbalance between the supplemental funds controlled by MCA and the existing programs controlled by a multitude of other agencies.[28]

These amendments to the bill, coupled with forceful lobbying by the administration, produced the desired results. On August 19 the Senate approved the bill by a comfortable margin of 53 to 22. The House passed the bill on October 14, after "one of the most acrimonious floor debates of the session."[29] And President Johnson signed the *Demonstration Cities and Metropolitan Development Act of 1966* (P.L. 89-754) on November 3, 1966. A week later Secretary Weaver rechristened the program "Model Cities" to avoid confusion with other types of "demonstrations" that were afflicting urban areas at the time.[30]

GUIDELINES FOR IMPLEMENTATION

In the final years of the Johnson administration the Great Society was on the wane, but enough time was left for it to make its imprimatur upon the beginnings of the Model Cities Program. As with most social legislation, the Model Cities Act contained a vague set of guidelines that HUD was expected to clarify and substantiate through administrative interpretation of congressional intent. By December of 1966, HUD had prepared a fifty-one-page *Program Guide* informing applicants for Model Cities grants of the program's operational requirements and outlining procedures for first-round funding applications.[31]

The cities selected were expected to participate in the program for approximately six years. The first year was to be devoted to planning, the product to be a Comprehensive Demonstration Plan (CDP). The CDP was to designate the specific content and objectives of programs to be implemented in the following year (called the first "action" year), and to set the general framework for programs over a continuing five-year period. It was anticipated that 150 cities would participate in this program, seventy-five to be selected for first-round funding in 1967 and seventy-five for second-round funding in 1968.

By the May 1, 1967 deadline for first-round funding, 193 cities had applied for Model Cities planning grants. Six months later sixty-three cities were selected to receive grants, and a few months after that twelve more cities were chosen, bringing to seventy-five the total number of planning grants awarded in the first round. The selection of participants was competitive, through a process in which applications were ranked by an intricate set of review and evaluation procedures designed by HUD, known as the Planning Grant Review Project. (Chapter 9).

Cities that applied for first-round planning grants followed the 1966 *Program Guide*, which required that applications include: (1) an analysis of the social, economic, and physical problems of the proposed Model Neighborhood Area; (2) a statement of the proposed program's goals, preferably quantified; (3) a general description of program approaches to be used; and (4) a description of the administrative machinery that would be employed to run the program. In 1967, HUD prepared a revised *Program Guide* for second-round applicants that emphasized the importance of problem analysis and methods for securing the involvement of local residents and agencies in the planning process rather than simply listing program proposals in the applications.[32]

Through the requirements set forth in these guides and other HUD documents, an operational definition of the Model Cities Program began to take shape. In regard to the program's target population, first-round applicants were informed merely that the Model Neighborhood Areas (MNAs, as the target areas were called) should be sizable, cohesive, and predominantly residential. Second-round applicants received more precise instructions from the 1967 *Program Guide*, which indicated that in large cities the MNA should contain no more than 10 percent of the population, with exceptions only where necessary for logical boundaries. Model Neighborhood Areas (MNAs) in small cities (under 150,000) were permitted to have populations of up to 15,000 and cities with less than 15,000 residents were allowed to designate the entire city as the MNA.

Both editions of the *Program Guide* reflected the statutory requirement that Model Cities planning be comprehensive in scope. Elaborating on this standard, components of a comprehensive approach were described by HUD as including: physical improvement, housing, transportation, education, manpower and economic development, recreation and culture, crime reduction, health, social services, and public assistance—although this list was to be considered "neither exhaustive nor directive."[33]

The objective of program innovation expressed in the Model Cities statute was also emphasized in administrative directives, mainly in the form of hortatory statements about new, imaginative approaches. Early in 1967, H. Ralph Taylor, HUD Assistant Secretary, noted: "The key to the demonstration approach to be used by the city is innovation . . . . An enlarged renewal program or a packaging or rearrangement of old programs will not do the job we contemplate. The program is intended to be a search for new paths to the local solution for local problems."[34] And later, the 1967 edition of the *Program Guide* called for "new," "imaginative," approaches and an "opportunity to experiment" in Model Cities, which directly reflects the language used in the preamble to the Model Cities Act.[35]

The development of innovative programs was to be supported by grants called supplemental funds, which were similar to bloc grants and could be used flexibly for a variety of Model Cities projects. Under the Model Cities statute, supplemental funds were to be used

> to assist new and additional projects and activities not assisted under a federal grant-in-aid program. To the extent such funds are not necessary to support fully such new and additional projects and activities, they may be used and credited as part or all of the required non-federal contribution to projects or activities assisted in a federal grant-in-aid program which are part of an approved comprehensive city demonstration program.[36]

A statutory formula determined the amount of supplemental funds to which a city was entitled. The formula allowed supplemental grants totalling up to 80 percent of the local share of categorical programs to be carried out in connection with the Model Cities Program. Thus, the more categorical program monies that were tied into the Model Cities plan, the greater the supplemental funds that a city would be eligible to spend on new activities. The objective of this formula was to provide an incentive for the coordination of federal programs with the Model Cities effort. One of the issues that arose in implementing this formula was whether only *new* categorical program activities initiated in conjunction with other Model Cities projects were to be included in the formula calculation or whether continuation grants for ongoing categorical programs (such as public assistance) were also eligible for inclusion. In addition, some members of Congress were afraid that if the distribution of supplemental funds was weighted on the basis of the availability of categorical grants, cities already accomplished in the art of "grantsmanship" would get the greatest benefits. On the other hand, those cities not already receiving categorical monies would find that their past failures worked against them in the competition for supplemental funds. To deal with some of the problems created by the legislative basis for allocation of supplemental funds, the formula was revised administratively by adding criteria of a city's need to calculate the amount of each city's grant (such as levels of poverty and amount of substandard housing). As it turned out, these need criteria became the major determinants of the size of the supplemental grant a city received.[37]

While supplemental funds were intended to be spent on innovative projects, a study analyzing their actual use reports:

> Contrary to the legislative priority given such use, most [Model Cities Programs] did not make substantial use of supplementary funds for new and additional (i.e., "innovative") projects which were not eligible for assistance under other federal grant programs. One of the most significant findings of the study was the amount of supplemental funds which were being used for projects which, with only minor modifications, would be legally eligible for funding with categorical funds.[38]

As envisioned by the Wood Task Force, the administrative machinery for Model Cities was to be tied firmly to local political leadership, whose support was required to accomplish program-coordination objectives. Speaking before a House subcommittee, Secretary Weaver was unequivocal in noting that each City Demonstration Agency (CDA), the organization that would run a local Model Cities Program, must "constitute a public body which is subject to the control of the local governing body."[39] HUD's instructions in the 1966 *Program Guide* followed the legislative proviso in specifying that the CDA "might be the city, the county, a public agency established expressly for the purpose, or an existing public agency." Elaborating on the intentions of this administrative structure, the instructions went on to note that the CDA should be clearly accountable to elected officials and "closely related to the governmental decision-making process in a way that permits the exercise of leadership by responsible elected officials in the establishment of the policies, plans, and activities of the local program."[40]

The Model Cities statute provided general directives that program planning should be based on local initiative, consider costs and benefits of alternative approaches, and result in comprehensive and innovative program designs. The planning methods for getting from "here to there" were not specified in the legislation. The planning process that cities were to follow in developing their Comprehensive Demonstration Plans (CDPs) was outlined by HUD in CDA Letter Number 4.[41] The HUD model was an ambitious attempt to get cities involved in a rigorous planning enterprise. This model stipulated that cities should engage in a rational, orderly, step-by-step approach in developing their CDPs. Initially, this entailed a three-part planning framework. Part I was to describe and analyze problems and their causes, to rank these problems in order of local priorities, and to indicate objectives, strategies, and program approaches to HUD two-thirds of the way through the planning year to allow for the feedback to the CDAs that would be useful for the completion of parts II and III. Part II was to be a statement of projected five-year objectives and cost estimates to achieve these objectives. This document was to be submitted at the end of the planning year with part III. Part III was to be a detailed statement of program plans for the first action year, the costs involved, and administrative arrangements for implementation. This document was to be a logical extension of the analysis, strategies, and priorities outlined in part I.

The demands this process made upon the cities' planning capacities is, perhaps, most clearly illustrated in Jordan's description of the expectations Model Cities Administration officials had of the problem analysis part of the planning:

> Problem analysis drew a lot of attention. It meant, MCA said, not just identification and description of problems in the Model Neighborhood and the lives of its citizens. It meant analyzing the *root causes* of the problems: the reasons they originated in the first place, the forces that maintain them. There was no depth limit set by Federal officials on problem analysis.[42] (Emphasis added.)

While the technical requirements of the planning process were elaborated in some detail in the HUD *Program Guide*, in the program's initial phase the sociopolitical aspects of the process were left largely to local determination. As previously noted, the major prescription the HUD *Program Guide* offered was that administrative and fiscal responsibility for the program be vested ultimately in the local chief executive. Beyond this, the initial guidelines left considerable latitude for the types of linkages and relationships among groups that might develop to imbue the decision making in development of the CDPs with an element of social choice as well as technical competence. Interpreting the statutory formula of "widespread citizen participation," the 1966 *Program Guide* noted that the CDA "should provide a meaningful role in policy making to area residents" as well as other groups expected to participate in the program; and it should create "mechanisms for a flow of communication and meaningful dialogue between the citizens of the area" and the CDA, and should afford opportunities for "area residents to participate actively in planning and carrying out the demonstration program as volunteers as well as wage earners."[43] The vagueness of these requirements ("meaningful roles" and "meaningful dialogues") allowed cities to create planning systems that varied widely in the degrees of decision-making influence given to citizen participants.

However, by 1967 pressures were developing within HUD to adopt a more expansive view of citizen participation. Staff for the Model Cities Administration (MCA) had been recruited largely from outside of HUD, and many of the key MCA personnel came from the Community Action Program of the Office of Economic Opportunity. These new staff were philosophically inclined to support strong citizen influence in local planning and decision-making processes. As James notes, it became apparent in early 1968 that there was a "generation gap between the initial sponsors of the legislation and many of those who would administer it," particularly in relation to issues of citizen participation.[44]

In addition to pressures from within the MCA, demands for greater citizen influence were also generated in the field. As neighborhood residents became involved in planning, struggles for power and control reminiscent of the Community Action Program erupted between citizen groups and CDAs. Warren attributes the unexpected momentum that citizen participation achieved, in part, to the prodding of the MCA staff but, more important, to the generalized phenomenon of the resident-participation movement that had taken root in the late 1950s and early 1960s.[45]

Under these mounting pressures from its own staff and the field, the MCA increased its emphasis on citizen influence in program development. Citizen participation requirements were tightened considerably in CDA Letter No. 3, *Citizen Participation*, dated October 1967, which designated six "performance standards":

1. There must be some form of organizational structure existing or newly established which embodies neighborhood residents in program planning and operation.
2. The leadership of that structure must consist of persons whom neighborhood residents accept as representing their interests.
3. The structure must have access to the CDA's decision-making process.
4. The structure must be provided information about pending decisions sufficiently in advance to be able to influence those decisions.

5. The structure must be provided professional technical assistance.
6. Where financial problems are a barrier to effective participation, neighborhood residents are to receive such assistance as will enable them to participate.[46]

These performance standards seemed to require a citizen participation structure independent of the CDA. They implied a model of advocacy planning wherein citizen groups would have their own planning staffs to develop and defend plans that reflected neighborhood interests as defined by citizens. Interpretation of these standards, however, varied at the regional level. Referring to a plan approved in one region that did not provide an independent citizens' structure, a HUD official in another region said, "We would not approve such a plan," and in fact every program in his region included an independent citizens' group.[47]

While local interpretations varied, the general trend encouraged by HUD was toward the development of independent citizen participation structures. By 1968, HUD was urging not only that technical assistance be made available to citizen groups, but that citizen groups be given a special budget for hiring their own staff of technicians independent of the CDAs.[48] Thus, in the final year of the Johnson administration, the guidelines for citizen participation embraced the concept of "advocacy planning," which, James noted, was forbidden to be mentioned at Model Cities Administration staff meetings in earlier years.[49]

During the Johnson administration's last month, nine cities that had completed the planning year were awarded grants for their first action year as the Democrats sought to firm up commitments and raise expectations that would make it difficult if not impossible for the incoming Nixon administration to abandon the program.

A SHIFT IN EMPHASIS: THE NEW FEDERALISM

One of George Romney's first acts as the new HUD Secretary was to cancel all nine Model Cities action grants approved by the outgoing administration in order to allow some time for the situation to be studied. On May 9, 1969, Secretary Romney released the first Model Cities action grants to Seattle, Atlanta, and Waco, Texas after announcing that the program was going to be reorganized along Nixonian lines. The salient objective of this proposed reorganization was to make Model Cities a mechanism for strengthening the planning and administrative capacity of general-purpose local government. This objective had implications for change that were directed both at citizen participation and at the role of the federal agencies in the Model Cities Program.

In regard to citizen participation, Secretary Romney expressed concern over the failure of the Johnson administration to establish guidelines that clearly awarded ultimate responsibility and authority for the program to local officials, and he promised to reaffirm this principle.[50] As one HUD official explained, "The message of this Administration is clear. The Model Cities Program is not to be controlled by citizen groups. Control and responsibility rest with local government."[51] This view of citizen participation was strongly expressed by Secretary Romney in a statement presented to the Subcommittee on Housing which was later incorporated into the citizen participation guidelines described in CDA Letter No. 10A. Shortly after Romney's statement, James reports: "One mayor called in his CDA citizen board and told its members to go home, they were no longer needed. However, this action was regarded as too drastic and he was encouraged to reverse that decision."[52]

Although the citizen participation requirements of CDA Letter No. 3 were not officially superseded, they were effectively diluted by the new guidelines. Thus, CDA Letter No. 10A stipulated: "The chief executive and the local governing body shall assume early, continuous, and ultimate responsibility for the development, implementation, and performance of the Model Cities Program."[53] In addition, CDA Letter No. 10B, dealing with citizen participation, made no mention of the earlier requirement that the leadership of the citizen participation structure be composed of persons accepted by neighborhoods as representing their interests, nor of the requirement that residents receive financial assistance when it was needed in order for them to participate.[54] And while CDA Letter No. 3 gave strong encouragement to development of an independent citizen participation structure controlled by residents, CDA Letter No. 10B stated: "This component shall be so structured as to afford fair representation to representatives of the residents of the Model Neighborhood, and to representatives of major elements of the city as a whole (e.g., religious, charitable, private, and public organizations) having an interest in the Model Neighborhood."[55]

By 1970, local communities began to experience the repercussions of the federal shift in emphasis on citizen participation. Local proposals to give citizen groups control over major parts of the program were resisted by HUD. For example, HUD required that the city of San Francisco maintain control over the major portion of its planning grant, in contrast to the 1968 approval of New Haven's proposal, which gave control of that city's entire planning grant to citizen participants.[56] HUD also rejected Philadelphia's Model Cities plan because it would have created several citizen-controlled nonprofit corporations to carry out parts of the program. These actions by HUD reflected policies issued in CDA Letter 10C and 10D, which limited the roles of both the CDA staff and citizen participation structures in operating ongoing projects; further, it limited the number of board members of any operating agency that could be appointed by the CDA staff or the citizen organization to one-third of total membership.[57] (In their analysis of the federal response to the Model Cities Program, Frieden and Kaplan note at several points that although the policy changes in the conduct of the program that we have mentioned did take place, the Nixon administration followed through on the financial commitments that had been made by the previous administration.)[58]

In addition to its renunciation of citizen participation and control at the neighborhood level, and consistent with its overall effort to strengthen the mayor's role in Model Cities, the Nixon administration sought to streamline program requirements and to delimit controls emanating from the federal level. One of the initial moves in this direction was aimed at the rigorous planning process that HUD required cities to follow. For many cities the demands of HUD's original planning model were too difficult to satisfy and they proved to be a source of frustration to mayors, CDA directors, and citizen groups. For example, the requirement that problem analyses dig all the way down to "root causes" encouraged tendencies toward infinite regression; with limited planning resources, five-year projection plans became exercises that merely diverted precious time and energy away from the important business of planning for the next year's program; and insistence on a comprehensive approach forced cities to mount thinly scattered efforts to analyze all of the major problems of Model Neighborhood Areas (MNAs) rather than allowing them to concentrate on the problems that they perceived to be most pressing. In retrospect, it appears that HUD's original planning model was overly ambitious, more responsive to the expectations of MCA's professional staff than to the planning capacities of most cities.

As previously noted, the original HUD process involved a three-part planning framework. Toward the end of 1969 this framework was simplified by elimination of the part II document (five-year objectives); reduction of the pressure to be comprehensive; and substitution of a Mid-term Planning Statement (limited to seventy-five pages) for the part I requirement. The Mid-term Planning Statement was to be revised at the end of the planning year and merged into the final Comprehensive Demonstration Plan.[59]

Although this simplification of the planning process represented a loosening of federal regulations, an elaborate system of federal guidelines and restraints still remained operative and was the subject of heavy criticism. In 1969 a Presidential Task Force on Model Cities, headed by Harvard Professor, Edward Banfield, was appointed. The Banfield Report, as it came to be known, was submitted to the White House on December 16, 1969 and was officially released September 10, 1970, accompanied by a statement that President Nixon in large measure supported its recommendations. The major thrust of the Banfield Report was its criticism of Model Cities for overregulation and undersupport. Commending the reduction and simplification of regulations that governed the planning process as a step in the right direction, the report went on to state:

> We must add, however, that in our opinion the cities are still nowhere near as free as they should be. They are still required to prepare too many documents according to specifications from Washington (in our opinion the full set of "guidelines," amounting to some 400 pages, which is 25% more than there were a year ago, should be reduced drastically), and they are still required to run too-long a gauntlet of review bodies before their proposals are approved and funded.[60]

Among its recommendations, the task force proposed that federal aid to cities take the form of a revenue-sharing plan that would substitute for many of the existing categorical grant-in-aid programs; it also proposed that Model Cities be continued, but that HUD's extensive reporting and review requirements be replaced by a single annual review to verify that each city was meeting certain basic requirements.[61]

Toward the end of 1970, the Nixon administration intensified efforts to reorganize Model Cities along the lines of the New Federalism. The president's revenue-sharing plan was in preparation. As presented to Congress in January, 1971, revenue sharing would have lumped funds for Model Cities, urban renewal, water and sewer grants, and rehabilitation loans into a $2 billion "urban development" fund to be distributed on a formula basis among 247 metropolitan areas. Only broad guidelines on the use of these grants were to be provided.[62] While the special-revenue-sharing proposal for urban development was not approved at that time,[a] Model Cities was used to test the basic strategy of revenue sharing. This experiment was called "Planned Variations."

---

[a]The proposal did come into being later, in *The Housing and Community Development Act of 1974* (Public Law 93-383, August 22, 1974) 42 U.S.C. 5301(c).[63]

In early statements outlining this experiment, Secretary Romney announced that the major variations would: eliminate all but statutorily defined federal reviews in cities; permit development of Model Cities plans and programs for entire cities rather than only for specific neighborhoods; and grant local chief executives the right to review, comment, and sign off on all federal categorical programs prior to their approval by federal agencies.[64]

Fifteen months later, the program's objectives had expanded from three to eight:

Planned Variation Program Objectives

1. Develop comprehensive plans for the entire city, not just the original and new Model Neighborhood Areas (MNAs), by using administrative, planning and evaluation funds on a citywide basis.
2. Coordinate the planning of federal programs through the local chief executive by utilizing the Chief Executive Review and Comment (CERC) procedure on major federal program activities.
3. Build the capacity of the local chief executive to budget resources and determine priority needs on a citywide basis by using administrative, planning and evaluation funds on a citywide basis.
4. Extend the impact of the Planned Variations funds to New Target Areas.
5. Increase local control of federal programs by reducing federal reviews and requirements and encouraging cities to request waivers.
6. Improve procedure for applying state resources and technical expertise to local needs by establishing State-Local Task Forces.
7. Develop a comprehensive and coordinated federal response to local needs by encouraging use of Regional Councils for Coordinating technical assistance and project funding.
8. Coordinate the delivery of HUD categorical programs to the locality in accordance with local priorities by negotiating an Annual Arrangement with each Planned Variation city.[65]

The aim of these variations was to shift the locus of allocative decision making within the federal-urban grant system to local executive leadership. The enhancement of the mayors' control over community planning was to be accomplished mainly through three of the variations. First, there was to be a reduction of federal reviews and requirements so that less discretion over the details of plans would be exercised at the federal level. At the same time, increased authority was delegated to the city level by way of the proposed procedure for chief executive review and comment (CERC). While the mayor's review and comment did not constitute a formal veto, it was intended to have substantially that effect. Skillfully employed, the

CERC could be a potent mechanism for the coordination of community planning under the mayor's office. Finally, the Model Cities were encouraged to enlarge their focus of planning from a neighborhood to a citywide basis. This citywide variation would increase the number of groups competing for programs, thus decreasing the influence that could be generated by any one neighborhood, and in effect strengthening the mayor's position in dealing with neighborhood groups.[66]

Planned Variations was a pilot effort for the revenue-sharing approach which the federal government undertook in the 1970s. With the development of this new approach, community planning veered off perceptibly from the course charted in the 1960s. Thus, while the Model Cities Program was not in itself an especially great success in eliminating poverty and reforming the federal categorical-grant system,[67] it did serve as a launching pad for some important new ideas. Model Cities was something of a success as a "demonstration," because it provided an opportunity for the country to experiment with some new methods of community planning.

Community planning in the 1970s is distinguished from planning in the 1960s by the development of new directions in funding arrangements that were begun with the Model Cities experience as well as by its main features concerning the relationships between citizen participants and local political leadership. Specifically, in the 1970s the role of local chief executives in community planning was considerably strengthened. At the same time, local political leaders were held increasingly accountable to their entire constituencies because elaborate federal requirements no longer served as a foil for local decision making. Citizen participation characterized by grassroots organizations, created in the Community Action Programs and Model Cities neighborhoods in the 1960s, were deemphasized. And as plans were designed to encompass a broader urban constituency, the actual influence of neighborhood groups diminished. Instead, the focus of political activity on the neighborhood level shifted from elected neighborhood councils and quasi-governmental citizen boards to the formal citywide political apparatus—injecting a new vitality into urban politics.

But the course is not clear. Few guidelines exist for the structures and processes that cities will create to plan the use of funds obtained through revenue sharing. As these changes move forward there is much to be gained by glancing backward to examine and reflect upon the recent community planning experiences out of which they emerged.

NOTES

1. For details of these historical developments see Alfred J. Kahn, *Theory and Practice of Social Planning* (New York: Russell Sage Foundation, 1969), pp. 23-24; Melvin Webber, "Comprehensive Planning and Social Responsibility," in *Urban Planning and Social Policy*, Bernard J. Frieden and Robert Morris, eds. (New York: Basic Books, Inc., 1968), pp. 9-10; William Alonso, "Critics, Planners, and Urban Renewal," *Urban Renewal: The Record and the Controversy* (Cambridge, Mass.: MIT Press, 1966), pp. 437-44; and Donald A. Schon and Thomas E. Nutt, "Endemic Turbulence: The Future for Planning Education," in *Planning in America: Learning from Turbulence*, David R. Godschalk, ed. (Washington, D.C.: American Institute of Planners, 1974), pp. 181-86.

2. Francine F. Rabinovitz, *City Politics and Planning* (New York: Atherton Press, 1969), p. 3.

3. For an historical account of these efforts, see Roy Lubove, *Community Planning in the 1920s: The Contribution of the Regional Planning Association of America* (Pittsburgh: University of Pittsburgh Press, 1963).

4. See Martin Anderson, *The Federal Bulldozer* (Cambridge, Mass.: MIT Press, 1964).

5. One of the best and most balanced assessments of urban renewal is offered by Charles Abrams, *The City is the Frontier* (New York: Harper and Row, 1965).

6. Peter M. Rossi and Robert Dentler, *The Politics of Urban Renewal* (New York: Free Press, 1961), pp. 287-88.

7. Scott Greer, *Urban Renewal and American Cities* (Indianapolis: Bobbs-Merrill, 1965), p. 37.

8. For example, see Kenneth B. Clark and Jeanette Hopkins, *A Relevant War Against Poverty* (New York: Harper and Row, 1968); Daniel P. Moynihan, *Maximum Feasible Misunderstanding* (New York: The Free Press, 1969); Sar A. Levitan, Garth L. Mangum, and Robert Taggart III, *Economic Opportunity in the Ghetto: The Partnership of Government and Business* (Baltimore: The Johns Hopkins Press, 1970); John Bibby and Roger Davidson, *On Capitol Hill: Studies in the Legislative Process* (New York: Holt, Rinehart and Winston, Inc., 1967).

9. Edward Banfield, "Revenue Sharing in Theory and Practice," *Public Interest*, 23, no. 2 (Summer 1969); 33-45.

10. Neil Gilbert, *Clients or Constituents* (San Francisco: Jossey Bass, 1970), pp. 52-53.

11. In addition to reference in note 18, see, Edward J. O'Donnel and Marilyn Sullivan, "Service Delivery and Social Action Through the Neighborhood Center: A Review of Research," *Welfare in Review* (November/December 1969): 1-2; Neil Gilbert, "Neighborhood Coordinator: Advocate or Middleman?" *Social Service Review* 43, no.: 2 (June 1969): 136-44; and Bernard J. Frieden and Marshall Kaplan, *The Politics of Neglect: Urban Aid from Model Cities to Revenue Sharing* (Cambridge, Mass.: MIT Press, 1975), pp. 99-125.

12. Lyndon B. Johnson, "President's Message on City Development," *Congressional Quarterly Weekly Report*, 4, February 1966, pp. 344-45.

13. Fred Jordan, "Model Cities in Perspective: A Selective History," in *Model*

Cities: A Report on Progress, special issue of Model Cities Center Service Bulletin (Washington,: Government Printing Office, 1971), p. 4)

14. For a detailed historical account of the background and development of the Model Cities Program at the national level see Frieden and Kaplan.

15. Judson L. James, "Federalism and the Model Cities Experiment," paper delivered at the 1970 Annual Meeting of the American Political Science Association, Los Angeles, September 1970, p. 2.

16. Simpson Lawson, "Programs: Wood Looks Back at the Checkered Past of Model Cities and Finch Says It Has A Future," *City* 3 (Fedruary 1969): 36.

17. James, p. 3.

18. U.S. House of Representatives, Committee on Banking and Currency, Subcommittee on Housing, *Demonstration Cities, Housing and Urban Development and Urban Mass Transit: Hearings*, 89th Congress, Session 2, 1966, p. 35.

19. Jordan, p. 6.

20. James, pp. 3-6.

21. In this section we have drawn on an excellent detailed account of the legislative history of the Demonstration Cities Act by Robert B. Semple, Jr., "Signing of Model Cities Bill Ends Long Struggle to Keep It Alive," *New York Times*, 4, November 1966.

22. U.S. House of Representatives, *Hearings*, p. 225.

23. Ibid., p. 98.

24. Gilbert, *Clients or Constituents*, pp. 6-9.

25. U.S. House of Representatives, *Hearings*, p. 3.

26. Semple, p. 1.

27. The $900 million authorized for supplemental funding of 150 model cities compares quite favorably to funding levels authorized in the Community Action program, which reached $1,980 billion in 1968 divided among approximately a thousand community action agencies.

28. James, p. 4.

29. *Congressional Quarterly Weekly Report*, 21, December 1966, p. 2585.

30. *New York Times*, 11, November 1966.

31. U.S. Department of Housing and Urban Development, *Improving the Quality of Urban Life: A Program Guide to Model Neighborhoods in Demonstration Cities*, December 1966, p. 47.

32. Ibid., December 1967.

33. Ibid., December 1966.

34. H. Ralph Taylor, "Model Neighborhoods and Demonstration Cities," *Michigan Municipal Review* 40 (March 1967): 62.

35. U.S. Department of Housing and Urban Development, *Program Guide*, December 1967, p. 4.

36. U.S. Congress, *Demonstration Cities and Metropolitan Development Act 1966*, P.L. 89-745, section 105(d).

37. U.S. Department of Housing and Urban Development, *The Federal Grant Process: An Analysis of the Use of Supplemental and Categorical Funds in the Model Cities Program* (Washington: D.C.: Government Printing Office, 1972), pp. 4-5.

38. Ibid., p. 1.

39. U.S. House of Representatives, *Hearings*, p. 36.

40. U.S. Department of Housing and Urban Development, *Program Guide*, December 1966, p. 11.

41. U.S. Department of Housing and Urban Development, *Comprehensive Planning Requirements in Model Cities*, CDA Letter No. 4, (Washington, D.C.: Government Printing Office, July 1968).

42. Jordan, p. 7.

43. U.S. Department of Housing and Urban Development, *Program Guide*, December 1966, pp. 11-14.

44. James, p. 6.

45. Warren, "Model Cities First Round," p. 248.

46. U.S. Department of Housing and Urban Development, *Citizen Participation*, CDA Letter No. 3, 30 October, 1967.

47. James Sundquist and David Davis, *Making Federalism Work* (Washington, D.C.: Brookings Institution, 1969), p. 92.

48. U.S. Department of Housing and Urban Development, *Citizen Participation*, Technical Assistance Bulletin No. 3 (December 1968).

49. James, p. 6.

50. *New York Times*, 29 April, 1969.

51. Ibid. 16 August, 1969.

52. James, p. 7.

53. U.S. Department of Housing and Urban Development, *Administrative Performance and Capability*, CDA Letter No. 10A, December 1969.

54. U.S. Department of Housing and Urban Development, *Joint HUD-OEO Citizen Participation Policy for Model Cities Programs*, CDA Letter No. 10B, March 1970.

55. Ibid., p. 2.

56. Richard LeGates, "Recent Developments in the Model Cities Program," *Clearinghouse Review* 4 (May 1970): 4-5.

57. U.S. Department of Housing and Urban Development, *Policy Statement on Economic Development*, CDA Letter No. 10C, November 1970; and HUD, *Separation of Responsibilities*, CDA Letter No. 10D, November 1970.

58. Frieden and Kaplan, pp. 223-31.

59. U.S. Department of Housing and Urban Development, *Submission Requirements for First Year Comprehensive Plans*, Memorandum from Floyd H. Hyde to All Second Round CDA Directors, 22 August, 1969.

60. President's Task Force on Model Cities, *Model Cities: A Step Toward the New Federalism* (Washington; D.C.: Government Printing Office, 1970), p. 9.

61. Ibid., pp. 10-15.

62. For further details, see Advisory Commission on Intergovernmental Relations, *Special Revenue Sharing: An Analysis of the Administrations Grant Consolidation Proposals* (Washingtin, D.C.: Government Printing Office, December 1971).

63. William Frej and Harry Specht, "The Housing and Community Development Act of 1974: Implications for Policy and Planning," *Social Service Review* 50, no. 2 (June 1976): 275-92.

64. U.S. Department of Housing and Urban Development, *HUD News*,

#70-723, "Statement by Secretary George Romney, September 30, 1970" (Washington; D.C.: Government Printing Office).

65. U.S. Department of Housing and Urban Development, Office of Community Development, *Planned Variations Evaluation Report* (Washington, D.C.: Government Printing Office, 1971).

66. For a more detailed analysis of Planned Variations see, Neil Gilbert, Armin Rosenkranz, and Harry Specht, "Dialectics of Social Planning," *Social Work* 18, no. 2 (March 1973): 78-86.

67. Frieden and Kaplan, pp. 99-125.

✳ **Chapter 2**

The Analytic Framework:
Propositions on Planning

This chapter describes the theoretical framework used for analysis of the dynamics of planning in the Model Cities Program from November 1967, when the first group of cities were selected, to the spring of 1971. By "analysis" we refer to an intellectual effort to divide a system into its constituent elements, to explain the relationships among these elements, and to understand how the system functions or meets its objectives. The first step in our analysis was to clarify the system's boundaries and its parts.

The systemic framework used to analyze community planning in Model Cities is illustrated in Figure 2-1. The planning system is divided into three levels: the *action system;* the *interorganizational field;* and the *community context.*

The *action system* is at the core of the planning framework; it focuses on the major sets of actors who actually did the planning for the Model Cities Program. Included here are the residents of the Model Neighborhood Area (MNA), the director of the City Demonstration Agency (CDA), and the professional staff of the CDA. These sets of actors and their relationships will be described in terms of:

1. *Demographic characteristics.* These characteristics include ethnicity of MNA residents, professionalism of CDA staff, and background and tenure of CDA directors.

2. *Structural arrangements.* The main element here is the type of administrative linkage between the CDA and the MNA citizen organization through which staff were provided to the citizen groups.

3. *Roles of CDA personnel.* The roles are described according to

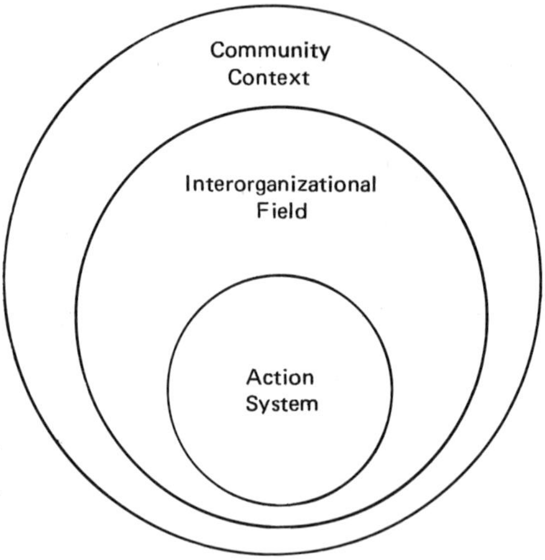

Figure 2-1. Planning System

the extent to which the CDA director's behavior was primarily technically oriented or primarily process oriented.

4. *Planning process.* The relationships among CDA staff and resident organizations formed the nucleus of local planning efforts. These relationships are described in terms of the degrees of influence that the CDA staff and the residents were able to exercise on decision making in the planning process. Specifically, three broad types of planning processes are identified: those in which CDA *staff influence* was the major determinant in decision making; those in which there was *parity* between CDA staff and resident groups in decision making; and those in which *resident influence* was the major determinant in decision making.

The next level of analysis focuses on the *interorganizational field* in which the action system is embedded. Community planning for Model Cities takes place in a field of public and private agencies that are concerned with the same problems, issues, and resources as the action system. In describing the elements in this field special attention is directed to the involvement of the city's chief executive (the city manager or mayor) and the degree to which he supported the Model Cities Program. In addition, we examine the numbers and types of other agencies that participated in planning in different communities, the degree to which their activities were coordinated, and the extent to which they committed funds to the Model Cities Program.

Finally, at the most inclusive level of analysis we focus upon the *community context*, within which both the interorganizational field and the action system operate. The major variables are: city size, per capita city budget, and prior planning experience in Model Cities-type programs.

Thus far we have outlined a static framework of various elements in the planning system. To comprehend the *dynamic* aspects of community planning we must, of course, consider how these elements relate to one another and how they affect the achievement of system objectives. The framework illustrated in figure 2-2 describes the relationships among the three levels of the planning system and Model Cities Program objectives that will be analyzed as we explore the dynamics of community planning.

As indicated in Figure 2-2, *process, product,* and *performance* are the three outcome measures related to elements at each level in the planning system. These outcomes were selected because they represent central objectives of the Model Cities program.

In this framework the *planning process* is treated as both a means and an end (as an independent and a dependent variable). As an end, it is perceived as an outcome of the action system. That is, one way of analyzing the action system is to study the types of planning process that occurred in different cities: staff influence, parity, or resident influence. At the same time the achievement of a "democratic" planning process, where local residents have major influence in determining programs for their neighborhoods, was valued by the

*Planning
System*   *Outcome*

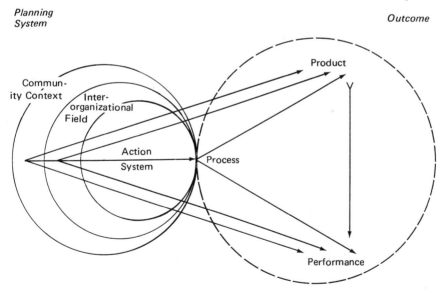

Figure 2-2. Framework for Analysis of Community Planning

Model Cities Administration as a means to achieve other Model Cities objectives.

The *product* refers to the Comprehensive Demonstration Plan (CDP), the formal documents submitted by Model Cities communities at the end of the planning period. The CDP contained proposals for programs to be implemented during the first action year, a detailed rationale for these programs, the administrative structure for implementation, and the amount of funds requested for support.

In addition, the CDP contained a statement of projected five-year objectives. As we indicated in chapter 1, the Model Cities Administration placed strong emphasis on the rational approach to local problem solving and the production of high-quality CDPs. The CDP had to be accepted and approved by HUD before communities could receive funding for the first action year.

While the stimulation of a democratic planning process and the development of quality planning documents were perceived as valuable objectives, the final test of the Model Cities Program was, of course, "getting things done," that is, implementing social and physical programs aimed at solving problems of urban decay and human strife. The objective of program *performance* refers to the degree of success that Model Cities communities experienced in their efforts to implement the programs they had planned.

Thus, the principal focus of this study is assessment of the degree to which the various elements we have identified in the planning system are associated with different types of planning processes that developed in Model Cities communities, variations in the quality of the CDPs that were produced, and different levels of performance in program implementation. In addition we analyze how process, product, and performance are related. Finally we examine the effort made by HUD to select systematically the most promising cities from among applicants for the Model Cities Program; this selection process was based on judgments by federal staff concerning each city's potential for achieving the program objectives.

The systems framework used in this analysis of community planning is a research orientation applicable to many phenomena. For example, consider a study of the automobile, a physical system that can be divided into three component parts: the outer shell, which offers protection, the steering apparatus, which allows for direction, and the motor, which provides propulsion. If we take safety as the performance criterion, it is possible to analyze how component elements of different automobiles contribute to this function by comparing, for instance: the construction, sturdiness, and weight of the outer shell; the responsiveness and stability of the steering apparatus; and the quickness of acceleration provided by the engine.

In this simplified example the reader will discern a certain arbitrariness concerning where the system boundaries are drawn and what is included. For instance, the engine might have been examined in terms of pistons, valves, and so forth. Various elements such as electrical circuits, radios, and other parts of the system were not separated out for study. And finally, factories that produce the spare parts and organizations that service the automobile were not defined within the system boundaries. We make this point to emphasize that in the systems approach the analyst must exercise a degree of discretion regarding the level of abstraction and units of analysis selected for investigation.[1] Similarly, another area of discretion involves the investigator's interpretation of the system functions. In our example the function of the system was to provide a *safe* ride. It might have been to provide a comfortable ride, an efficient ride, or a ride that does not befoul the environment. The number of possibilities is enormous, and the investigator struggles to discriminate among stated objectives, real objectives, and legitimate objectives.[2] If advertisements are any indication, one could argue that the function of the automobile are to confer sex appeal, status, and happiness on its owner.

The automobile example illustrates some of the choices that confront analysts using the systems approach with relatively concrete phenomena. These choices multiply when studying complex social systems such as urban communities. Thus, in the Model Cities study we faced the choice of where to draw boundaries, and the lines were not always self-evident. At the inner core, it might be argued, the chief executive should fall within the action system rather than the interorganizational field. This is a logical possibility. We chose the interorganizational field alternative because, unlike the CDA and Model Neighborhood resident organization, the chief executive's major responsibilities and administrative activities typically extend far beyond the Model Cities Program. Other agencies and programs throughout the city demand his loyalty and concern, some of which may not be in harmony with the objectives of the CDA. Similarly, at the outer boundary of the planning system we did not include HUD personnel. The analysis of federal-local relationships in the Model Cities Program is both interesting and important, but that would have required a different study.

In addition to drawing boundaries, our analysis of the forces and processes that affect community planning had to be selective regarding the many variables and relationships within the planning system. How does one begin to study a nationwide program as varied and complex as Model Cities? What factors should be selected for investigation out of the myriad possibilities? Why? In presenting the analytic framework we have already described the factors selected for this study. For the most part, what prompted their selection was our ambition to examine, on a large-scale empirical basis, what is known and what is thought to be known about important elements in the dynamics of community planning. That ambition was constrained by feasibility of measurement. As we thought about constructing the analytic framework, various assumptions and propositions informed our selection of elements and relationships in the planning system.

Some of these propositions come from the realm of conventional wisdom about felicitous combinations of valued means and desired outcomes that are believed to have strong connections because the world is more comprehensible and benign under these circumstances. An example of such a proposition is the belief that strong citizen influence in planning and decision making will be associated with a high level of performance in program implementation. However, this proposition has been the subject of few systematic attempts at empirical verification, except perhaps indirectly and under the quite limited conditions of the small-group laboratory.[3] Other propositions come from the social science literature on community planning in which the logical derivation and rationale are more rigorously developed and accompanied by empirical evidence.

At this point we will not attempt to explicate the rationale for the choice of every variable and relationship analyzed in this study. In some cases the rationale will be relatively self-evident, and in others it will be discussed in the body of the text, particularly in part III. However, to provide a general orientation and background to the genesis of this study, some of the main propositions that guided our choice of the elements in planning will be illustrated in the following discussion of variables in the action system, the interorganizational field, and the community context.

PROPOSITIONS ON THE ACTION SYSTEM

In recent years probably no element of community planning has generated greater interest or received more investigation than the decision-making relationships between resident groups and community planning agencies such as City Demonstration Agencies (CDAs), Community Action Agencies (CAAs), and Urban Redevelopment Authorities (URAs).[4] Most of the research about citizen participation have been case studies that cover a limited number of cities or neighborhoods. In the main, these studies document the inability of citizen participation to influence program decision making. Yet, in scattered cases citizen participation was a dominant force in the planning process. In general the evidence on citizen participation is consistent with the overall findings of our study, which indicate that in only a small proportion (18 percent) of the Model Cities was citizen participation a dominant factor in decision making, while in the majority of cases (56 percent) CDA staff was the dominant influence.

To analyze the dynamics of community planning at the level of the action system, we must go beyond these descriptive categories and attempt to explain the presence of variation, those "odd" cases where citizen influence was dominant. Thus, we will examine the degree to which different elements in the action system are associated with the development of alternative patterns of resident influence in the Model Cities planning process. And we will also compare how alternative patterns of influence are associated with different levels of program performance. In this analysis our selection of variables and relationships to analyze was guided (though not exclusively determined) by the following five propositions. We have intentionally stated each proposition in as simple and brief a form as possible without probing some of the inherent complexities and difficulties of operationally defining key variables. We will take up this point in the last section of this chapter.

Proposition 1: The degree of citizen influence in the Model Cities planning process will vary directly with the proportion of minority residents in the target area (Model Neighborhood Area, or MNA). In the 1960s there was a growing resolve among minority groups to exercise proportional influence in community affairs, which in many cases meant to control the institutions in their neighborhoods. According to Rothman et al., a review of the research on participation indicates that "poor white communities showed the lowest participation in community action programs;" and "a limited amount of client participation is associated with less impact on agency decision-making."[5] The proposition is also supported by Mogulof's observation on the Model Cities Program:

> Based upon the experience to date, one can speculate on the further diffusion and acceleration of changes in black-dominated neighborhoods within the Model Cities Program. Very probably these changes will see neighborhood councils or congresses emerge as quasi-governmental units for their areas. . . . These neighborhood groups will be given their own staff resources with which to develop their own program plans, and with which to refine and counter plans drawn for their neighborhoods by other sectors of the community.[6]

In contrast to the above findings, a review of citizen participation research by Yin et al. indicates that racial homogeneity in the target neighborhood was *not* strongly associated either positively or negatively with successful citizen influence. However, it is noted in this study that because of the composition of the sample cases these results should be taken only as suggestive.[7]

Proposition 2: The degree of citizen participation in the Model Cities planning process will be inversely related to the size of the population in the Model Neighborhood Area. This proposition is drawn from the findings of Yin et al. In their study of fifty-one cases of citizen participation they found that citizen influence was effective more often where the target population was less than 20,000.[8]

Proposition 3. The more control the citizen organization has in hiring its own staff, the greater will be its influence in the decision-making process. The structure of community planning programs, especially the staffing links between the planning agency and the citizen organization, is believed to be crucial to the type of planning process that will emerge. Arnstein states:

> Partnership can work most effectively when there is an organized power-base in the community to which the citizen leaders are accountable; when the citizens' group has the financial resources to pay its leaders reasonable honoraria for their time-consuming efforts; and when the group has the resources to hire (and fire) its own technicians, lawyers, and community organizers. With these ingredients, citizens have some genuine bargaining influence over the outcome of the plan (as long as both parties find it useful to maintain the partnership).[9]

A few pages later in the same planning journal, Warren notes:

> The growth of resident strength is indicated by the amount of funding available to various Model Neighborhood boards to engage their own planning staffs who are responsible to them rather than depending on planning staff parcelled out from the Model Cities Agency or from some other community decision organization.[10]

Finally, Yin et al. report that significant implementation of citizen views occurred in 33 percent more cases when the citizen organization had staff under its own control than under other staffing arrangements.[11]

Proposition 4: The more technical (rather than political) the role orientation of the CDA planner, the less likely that citizen influence will be dominant in the decision-making process. The first two propositions address the impact of client groups and the structure of the resident organization on the decision-making process. While the professional planner in the action system responds to the forces generated by clients and structure, his role, in turn, affects the type of decision-making process that emerges.[12]

In most of the literature on community planning, the planner's role is discussed from one or both of two perspectives: technical functions (or task orientation) and sociopolitical functions (or process orientation). The traditional view of the community planner's role has emphasized the performance of a combination of technical tasks such as data collection, problem analysis, ranking priorities, program design, cost-benefit analysis and model building, and the like. As Hollander puts it:

> What planners should have in common, regardless of origins and special orientations, are the minimum levels of competence in using the planners' tools. The discipline of planning should focus on these tools. I fear that a broader role for the discipline will dissipate efforts to the point that essential gaps in methodology will not be filled.
>
> This is not to suggest that the planner is simply a technician; on the contrary, his perspective must be broad, his talents many, and his education interdisciplinary; *but competence in the methodology of his profession is the source of his power and his influence.*[13] (Emphasis added.)

More recently, a second perspective on the planner's role, which involves a sociopolitical dimension, has been prominent in the literature.[14] From this perspective the planner is seen as performing a combination of interactional tasks such as structuring a planning system, advocating his client's interest, and facilitating communication, bargaining, and exchange among relevant parties to the planning decisions. Few authorities on planning would deny the relevance of both functions, though opinion on the degree to which they are or should be emphasized might differ. In general these technical and sociopolitical functions are viewed either as complimentary facets of the planner's role or at least as not mutually exclusive.[15] Hence, in proposition 4 we refer to the planner's "role orientation" because the technical-sociopolitical distinction is more one of degree than kind. In terms of the degree to which one or another of these role orientations is emphasized, planners' roles have been described using various labels such as technocrat, bureaucrat, and advocate.[16] In an empirical study of city planning, Rabinovitz has analyzed the extent to which the planning roles of technician, broker, and mobilizer are associated with effectiveness. She found that the technician role functioned most effectively in a cohesive community where the patterns of influence were relatively stable.[17] The application of this finding to the Model Cities Program would suggest that CDA planners with a technical role orientation would be inclined to favor working within existing power arrangements and disinclined to encourage the development of new centers of influence in citizen organizations.

Proposition 5: The greater the degree of citizen influence in the planning process, the higher the level of performance in program implementation. We have already noted that this proposition rests in part upon findings from small group research.[18] In addition, Yin et al. conclude that, from the few systematic efforts made to study the impact of citizen participation on program effectiveness, more often than not citizen participation appears to have positive effects on program effectiveness. However, the data presented to support this point are equivocal.[19]

The case is generally made that when people participate directly in determining policies that affect their lives, the decisions are more likely to produce support and commitment than when policies are determined for them. In the context of the Model Cities Program this would suggest that in communities where citizen influence was weak during the planning phase, local support and commitment required for program implementation was difficult to muster. This proposition has special significance because citizen participation is not simply a means to facilitate program implementation, but also a valued end in its own right: this dual character of citizen participation can pose some perplexing choices for the planning enterprise if proposition 5 cannot be verified. However, it should be emphasized that this is not a zero-sum proposition, but one that addresses the issues of the *degree* of citizen participation associated with each different level of program performance.

PROPOSITIONS ON THE INTERORGANIZATIONAL FIELD

It is a commonplace observation in interorganizational studies that, in order to survive, an organization must establish cooperative relationships and exchanges with other elements in its environment. These "other elements" are variously defined. For example, they are conceptualized broadly by Warren in terms of "input constituencies" (groups that perform supporting functions, to whom the organization is accountable) and "output constituencies" (the target groups or consumers of the organization's services).[20] Similarly, Dill identifies those parts of the environment upon which an organization's goal achievement is potentially dependent as: clients or customers; suppliers of needed resources such as funds, staff, and equipment;

competitors; and regulatory groups. Taken together, these elements constitute what he calls the "task environment."[21] An organization's claim to its sphere of activity, purpose, and objectives is substantiated through interaction with the task environment. Thompson sums it up:

> The establishment of domain cannot be arbitrary, unilateral action. Only if the organization's claims to domain are recognized by those who can provide the necessary support, by the task environment, can a domain be operational. The relationships between an organization and its task environment is essentially one of exchange, and unless the organization is judged by those in contact with it as offering something desirable, it will not receive the inputs necessary for survival.[22]

Applying these observations to the Model Cities Program, we can anticipate that an organization that stakes out a broad claim to do comprehensive planning, such as the CDA, will have unsettling effects on the interorganizational field. That is, the Model Cities contained numerous organizations whose activities and objectives involved planning to improve the physical environment and to enhance social welfare. Over time these organizations had negotiated a consensus about which activities were in each organization's domain. With the advent of the Model Cities Program and the creation of the CDA, a new disruptive element is added to the interorganizational field. This would parallel the development found in Rose's study of the Community Action Program:

> When a new organization brings with it an unclear set of domain expectations, regulations insisting on new participants in the local game, and undetermined methods of organizational interaction, the domain consensus within the community is unsettled. This was clearly the case with the Community Action Program. . . . The comprehensive thrust of the antipoverty effort involved itself immediately in the domain concerns of every service system.[23]

In examining the interorganizational field of the Model Cities Program we focused upon participation of public and private agencies related to Model Cities objectives and the role of the local chief executive. Using Warren's terminology, these elements may be considered major "input constituencies." Our analysis seeks to reveal the extent to which the relationships between the CDA and these elements of the task environment are associated with citizen influence in the planning process and with program implementation. In the selection of the variables and relationships to be analyzed we were guided by the following two major propositions.

Proposition 6: The larger the number of public and private agencies participating in the Model Cities planning, the weaker the degree of citizen influence in the planning process. The CDA presented both an opportunity and a threat to public and private agencies in its task environment. The opportunity was to obtain new federal funds. As a new source of funds, the CDA's intrusion upon local domains was not entirely unwelcome. The threat was that through the involvement of citizen organizations in planning and decision making, local agency autonomy would be considerably reduced. While agencies might be inclined to renegotiate the existing domain consensus to share power with the CDA, they would be less inclined to do this if it also meant they had to include local citizen organizations that probably contained (or at least represented) their clients and whose demands were relatively unpredictable. Power-sharing relationships with citizen organizations through the CDA threatened not only to decrease agency autonomy but, perhaps more important, to increase uncertainty in their task environment. The agencies' responses to the opportunity presented by the CDA would depend in large measure upon how much they perceived the trade-off to cost in terms of their autonomy and upon the degree of uncertainty in the field. The proposition suggests that for many agencies the trade-off costs would be considered too high if citizen influence in the planning process was very strong. This is consistent with Rose's findings that, in the Community Action Program, relationships between the Community Action Agency and local agencies tended to reinforce the existing domain consensus.[24]

Proposition 7: The degree of chief executive support for the Model Cities Program will be directly associated with the level of performance in program implementation. Often, the implementation of community planning involves the allocation of resources among diverse and competing interest groups. This translation of plans into programs requires not only technical and administrative skill, but also the sanction and power to mediate and, if necessary, override competing claims when an impasse threatens. The local chief executive is usually the most prominent source for both sanction and power to implement plans. In her study of city planning agencies Rabinovitz observes that:

> since the 1940's there has been a pronounced trend away from the independent planning commission and toward agencies within the municipal bureaucracy. This change was probably spurred by theories showing that the executive structure provided a compelling answer to the problems of implementing city plans. The theories indicate that this structure was able to realize that plans not having political support are likely to be ineffectual.[25]

While evidence from the literature in support of this proposition is strong, it is not entirely one-sided. For example, in the introduction to his analysis of mayoral influence in urban policy making, Kuo notes that many studies tend to present the mayor as "a political actor of limited power" responding mainly to the dictates of business groups or to pressures from other powerful groups in the community.[26] However, Kuo's findings run contrary to his weak-mayor hypothesis. His study, based on data collected from ninety-three cities, indicates that the adoption of community programs was directly related to the degree of mayoral support they received.[27] Similarly, Rosenthal and Crain, in a survey of 1186 cities, found that local chief executive support was a major factor in the outcome of decisions concerning fluoridation.[28] Finally, and closer to the subject, a Department of Health, Education and Welfare study of the integration of services in thirty communities, indicates that one of the most important factors facilitating services integration was "support from the external sociopolitical environment in which the project functioned."[29]

In the Model Cities Program, local chief executive support was a prerequisite to funding. Hence, at least initially, all the participating cities had local chief executives who indicated a positive interest in the program. While they were not directly engaged in the daily business of Model Cities planning, local chief executives had the responsibility to guide, mediate, and exercise final authority over the program. The extent to which they fulfilled this responsibility varied. This proposition suggests that the implementation of Model Cities plans will reflect the degree to which the local chief executive's initial interest was followed up by an active role in the program. When we compare the data on this proposition with data on proposition 5 (which suggests a direct relationship between citizen participation and program implementation), we can derive some insight into the relative impact of different constituencies on CDA functioning. Citizen organizations in the Model Cities field represent an overlapping of input and output constituencies, while the local chief executive is clearly an input constituency. According to Warren, planning organizations respond more strongly to the interests and concerns of their input constituencies.[30] Thus, we might expect that a high degree of chief executive support would have a greater influence on program implementation than a high degree of citizen participation.

PROPOSITIONS ON THE COMMUNITY CONTEXT

To fully understand the dynamics of Model Cities operations they must be seen in a larger context than the Model Neighborhood Area (MNA), the target for planning and program implementation. The MNAs were parts of cities and towns ranging in size from 2300 to 8,000,000. Studies of community planning from a macroperspective invariably include city size as one of the major variables associated with planning processes and outcomes. In addition to size, the historical community planning experiences of these cities and towns provide a reservoir of skills and knowledge that could serve the entire community and is, therefore, relevant to the Model Cities Program whether or not such experiences occurred in the MNA. The social climate of these cities and towns during the turbulent 1960s also must be taken into account in explaining the forms of planning that emerged in the MNAs.

Size, experience, and other properties of the larger community will be examined to determine the relationship between community context and how the Model Cities Program functioned. In this analysis we were guided by the following three propositions.

Proposition 8: City size will be positively associated with the degree of citizen participation in planning and decision making. The available empirical evidence on this proposition is contradictory. Austin's study of the antipoverty program indicates that active citizen participation (relatively successful in exercising influence) was found more frequently among Community Action Agencies in larger cities (over 150,000) than in smaller cities.[31] Yin et al., on the other hand, found that citizen participation organizations in a variety of programs (including Model Cities) overall were less successful in exercising influence in larger cities (over 250,000) than in smaller cities.[32] Of course, this proposition does not imply that the degree of citizen participation is directly a function of such global property as city size. Many intervening variables associated with size might account for the proposed relationship.

Proposition 9: City size will be positively associated with levels of performance in program implementation. Here too the evidence is contradictory. Differing theoretical explanations are found in the literature to show why large cities are either more likely or less likely to achieve high levels of performance in program implementation. For example, based on a study of desegregation in fifty-one cities, Dye argues that the larger cities were less successful in implementing policy, partly because larger cities tend to be more bureaucratic than smaller cities. In brief, this point of view assumes that complexity and greater structural differentiation of larger cities lead to more bureaucratized arrangements, the general inflexibility of which are obstacles to the implementation of new policies.[33] However, studies by Aiken and Alford on the implementation of public housing and urban renewal programs reveal strong positive correlations between city size and program implementation.

First, larger cities are likely to have more organizations devoted to specific kinds of decision-areas, i.e., more likely to have a redevelopment agency, a housing agency, a community action agency. . . . Such organizations are likely to have larger, more specialized, and more professional staffs to provide the technical, administrative, and political knowledge required to innovate successfully, not only within their organizations, but also in the activation of interorganizational relationships and establishment of critical coalitions. Second, it is precisely in the larger, more structurally differentiated communities that coalitions that can implement an innovation will be easiest to establish. If we assume that only a limited number of organizational units need to be mobilized to bring about a successful innovation, then it follows that in large, highly differentiated communities a lower proportion of the available organizations will participate in such decisions, and that there will be wider latitude in selecting organizations for these critical coalitions.[34]

To summarize, the issue is whether the greater bureaucratization that accompanies structural differentiation in large cities is an obstacle to program implementation because the various bureaucracies tend to develop domain consensus and to become firmly set in their ways. An alternative hypothesis is that the higher degrees of bureaucratization in large cities is an asset because the more bureaucracies (centers of influence) available, the smaller the proportion of the overall system required to obtain a "critical mass" of support for program implementation.

Proposition 10: The degree of prior experience in community planning programs (such as urban renewal and public housing) will be positively associated with levels of performance in the Model Cities Program. This proposition is derived from the Aiken and Alford studies of implementation in public housing and urban renewal programs. In addition to city size (structural differentiation), they suggest that one of the properties that contributes to a community's capacity to implement new programs is the accumulation of experience and information. In their studies they infer this property from the city's age. As they explain:

Presumably older cities have had a longer time for existing organizations to have worked out patterns of interaction, alliances, factions, or coalitions. In such communities the state of knowledge in the community system about the orientations, needs, and probable reactions to varying proposals for community action is likely to be quite high, thus increasing the proba-bility of developing a sufficiently high level of coordination in order to implement successfully a community innovation. [35]

In our analysis of the Model Cities Program (which is of relatively recent origin compared to public housing and urban renewal), rather than using a city's age as the indicator of knowledge and experience it has accumulated related to urban planning, we employ what would seem to be a more direct measure: the length of the city's experience in urban renewal and public housing programs. Thus, for example, we take into account the fact that over the last decade cities have used urban renewal programs not only to secure federal funds for themselves, but also to create, outside the city's regular departmental structure, a cadre of professional talent that could be employed in various capacities. "The best local renewal authorities," Wilson ob-serves, "became generalized sources of innovation and policy staffing and their directors became in effect deputy mayors (and sometimes more than that)."[36]

CONCLUSION

Our list of propositions on community planning is partial, but it illustrates some of the theoretical guideposts of our investigation. In the studies cited, different phrases or concept labels are used to convey the same meaning. For example, Austin uses "active partici-pation," Yin et al. use "program impact," and we use "degree of citizen influence" to identify essentially the same phenomenon: the extent to which citizen groups were able to wield power and to influence decision making. In this brief review we converted some of the concepts or theoretical variables in the studies cited into the standard terms used in this study.

However, we were unable to standardize the distance between these concepts or theoretical variables and the empirical indicators used to represent them. The research cited involved case studies, surveys, secondary analyses of case study data, and other techniques that place the investigator at varying distances from the phenomena being studied. Moreover, the precise operational definitions of even relatively concrete variables, such as "large" and "small" cities, dif-fered. These differences are not merely a reflection of rampant indi-vidualism among scholars; rather, the differences reflect some of the difficulties of attempting to approximate measurements of the complex subject matter under investigation. In the literature on community planning, similar meanings are inferred from diverse indicators. It is, therefore, important that these indicators be made explicit.

NOTES

1. For a concise review of the literature that identifies social system models according to levels of abstraction and component units, see Robert Mayer, "Social System Models for Planners," *Journal of the American Institute of Planners*, 38, no. 3 (May 1972): 130-39.

2. These choices are discussed in C. West Churchman, *The Systems Approach* (New York: Dell Publishing Co., 1968), pp. 28-60.

3. For example, see Ralph White and Ronald Lippitt, "Leader Behavior and Member Reaction in Three Social Climates," *Group Dynamics: Research and Theory*, eds. Dorwin Cartwright and Alvin Zander (New York: Harper and Row, 1960); and Jacob Levine and John Butler, "Lecture vs. Group Decision in Changing Behavior," *Journal of Applied Psychology* 36 (February 1952): 29-33.

4. For a representative sampling of the vast literature in this area, see Ralph Kramer, *Participation of the Poor* (Englewood Cliffs, N.J.: Prentice-Hall, Inc., 1969); Peter Rossi and Robert Dentler, *The Politics of Urban Renewal* (New York: Free Press, 1961); James Q. Wilson, "Planning and Politics: Citizen Participation in Urban Renewal," *Urban Renewal: People, Politics and Planning*, eds. Jewel Bellush et al. (New York: Anchor Books, 1967); Neil Gilbert, *Clients or Constituents* (San Francisco: Jossey Bass, Inc., 1970); Arthur B. Shostak, "Promoting Participation of the Poor: Philadelphia's Anti-Poverty Program," *Social Work* 11, no. 1 (1966); Stephen Rose, *The Betrayal of the Poor: The Transformation of Community Action* (Cambridge,: Schenkman Publishing Co., 1972); Kenneth Pollinger and Annette Pollinger, *Community Action and the Poor* (New York: Praeger Publishers, 1972); "Maximum Feasible Manipulation" as told to Sherry Arnstein by the North City Area Wide Council, Inc., *City* (October-November 1970); Michelle Osborn, "Postscript: Philadelphia's Model Cities Conflict in Context," *City* (October-November 1970); Kenneth B. Clark and Jeannette Hopkins, *A Relevant War Against Poverty: A Study of Community Action Programs and Observable Social Change* (New York: Harper and Row, 1969); Edward M. Kaitz and Herbert Harvey Hyman, *Urban Planning for Social Welfare: A Model Cities Approach* (New York: Praeger Publishers, 1970); Roland Warren, "Model Cities First Round: Politics, Planning, and Participation," *Journal of the American Institute of Planners* 35, no. 4 (July 1969): 245-52; Department of Housing and Urban Development, *The Model Cities Program: A Comparative Analysis of the Planning Process in Eleven Cities* (Washington, D.C.: Government Printing Office, 1970); Jon Van Til and Sally Bould Van Til, "Citizen Participation in Social Policy: The End of the Cycle?" *Social Problems* 17, no. 3 (Winter 1970); and *Community Representation in Community Action Programs*, Study Director, David Austin, Florence Heller Graduate School for Advanced Studies in Social Welfare, Brandeis University, report No. 1 (February 1968).

5. Jack Rothman et al., *Guidelines for Social Change: Utilization of Social Science Research in Social Planning and Community Action* (interim draft), January 1972, University of Michigan (mimeo.).

6. Melvin Mogulof, "Coalition to Adversary: Citizen Participation in Three Federal Programs," *Journal of the American Institute of Planners* 35, no. 4 (July 1969): 230-31.

7. Robert K. Yin et al., *Citizen Organization: Increasing Client Control Over Services* (Santa Monica, Calif.: RAND Corp. 1973), p. 49.

8. Ibid., p. 51.

9. Sherry Arnstein, "A Ladder of Citizen Participation," *Journal of the American Institute of Planners* 35, no. 4 (July 1969): 221-22.

10. Roland Warren, "Model Cities First Round: Politics, Planning, and Participation," *Journal of the American Institute of Planners* 35, no. 4 (July 1969): 247.

11. Yin et al., p. 59.

12. For a cogent discussion of client-planner relationships, see Richard S. Bolan, "The Social Relations of the Planner," *Journal of the American Institute of Planners* 37, no. 6 (November 1971): 386-96.

13. Theodore E. Hollander, "How Encompassing Can the Profession Be?" *Urban Planning in Transition*, ed. Ernest Erber (New York: Grossman Publishers, 1970), p. 149.

14. For example, see Paul Davidoff, "Advocacy and Pluralism in Planning," *Journal of the American Institute of Planners* 31, no. 4 (November 1965): 331-38.

15. The different tasks associated with the technical and sociopolitical aspects of planning are discussed in Ralph Kramer and Harry Specht, eds., *Readings in Community Organization Practice* (Englewood Cliffs, N.J.: Prentice-Hall, Inc., 1969), pp. 8-12; Robert Perlman and Arnold Gurin, *Community Organization and Social Planning* (New York: John Wiley and Sons, 1972), pp. 52-75; and Neil Gilbert and Harry Specht, *Planning for Social Welfare* (Englewood Cliffs, N.J.: Prentice-Hall, 1977), pp. 147-391.

16. Neil Gilbert and Harry Specht, *Dimensions of Social Welfare Policy* (Englewood Cliffs, N.J.: Prentice-Hall, Inc., 1974), pp. 186-187.

17. Francine Rabinovitz, *City Politics and Planning* (New York: Atherton Press, 1969).

18. See note 4.

19. Yin et al., pp. 41-45.

20. Roland Warren, "The Interaction of Community Decision Organizations: Some Basic Concepts and Needed Research," *Social Service Review* 41, no. 3 (September 1967).

21. William Dill, "Environment as an Influence on Managerial Autonomy," *Administrative Science Quarterly* 2 (March 1958): 409-43.

22. James D. Thompson, *Organizations in Action* (New York: McGraw Hill, 1967), p. 28. This slim volume is a rich source of propositions on organizational behavior.

23. Rose, pp. 164-65.

24. Ibid., op. pp. 168-70.

25. Rabinovitz, p. 40.

26. Wen H. Kuo, "Mayoral Influence in Urban Policy Making," *American Journal of Sociology* 79, no. 3 (November 1973): 620. In support of the weak-mayor hypothesis, Kuo cites: Floyd Hunter, *Community Power Structure* (Chapel Hill: University of North Carolina Press, 1953) and Peter H. Rossi, "The Organizational Structure of an American Community," *Complex Organizations*, ed. Amitai Etzioni (New York: Holt, Rinehart, and Winston, 1965).

27. Kuo concludes from his analysis: "The behavior of the mayor in urban policy making tended to influence the fate of a proposed program. Whenever he failed to act in behalf of a program, either in its initiation or in its promotion, the chances that the program would be rejected increased" (Kuo, p. 637).

28. Donald Rosenthal and Robert Crain, "Executive Leadership and Community Innovation," *Urban Affairs Quarterly* 1 (March 1966): 39-57.

29. U.S. Department of Health, Education and Welfare, *Integration of Human Services in HEW: An Evaluation of Service Integration Projects*, vol. 1 (Washington, D.C.: Government Printing Office, 1972), p. 46.

30. Warren.

31. David M Austin, "Resident Participation: Political Mobilization or Organizational Co-optation," *Public Administration Review* 32 (September 1972): 409-20.

32. Yin et al., pp. 50-51.

33. Thomas Dye, "Urban School Segregation: A Comparative Analysis," *Urban Affairs Quarterly* 4 (December 1968): 141-65.

34. Michael Aiken and Robert R. Alford, "Community Structure and Innovation: The Case of Urban Renewal," *American Sociological Review* 35, no. 4 (August 1970): 662; also see Michael Aiken and Robert Alford, "Community Structure and Innovation: The Case of Public Housing," *American Political Science Review* 64, no. 3 (September 1970): 843-64; and Terry Clark, "Urban Typologies and Political Outputs: Causal Models Using Discrete Variables and Orthogonal Factors, or Precise Distortion Versus Model Muddling," *Social Science Information* 9, no. 6 (December 1970): 7-33.

35. Michael Aiken and Robert Alford, "Community Structure and Innovation: The Case of Public Housing," *American Political Science Review* 64, no. 3 (September 1970); 863.

36. James Q. Wilson, "The Mayors Versus the Cities," *The Public Interest* 23, no. 3 (Summer 1969): p. 30.

✳ Chapter 3

Methods: Indicators and Measurements
of Community Planning

As is often the case in social research on action programs, many of the Model Cities variables that appeared to be most important and interesting (power, influence, conflict, support, and success of implementation) were also extremely complex and difficult to measure in quantitative form. The nature of this problem is cogently expressed in Durkheim's observation that to grasp elusive social phenomena we must substitute for the internal fact which escapes us an external fact that represents it, and thus, study the former through the latter.[1]

However, in the Model Cities Program even many of the external facts have an elusive quality. For example, the degree of citizen influence might be studied by reference to external facts such as how often decisions were made that favored the citizen group position when there was disagreement among parties. To have done this would have required analyzing many of the decisions made in 147 communities over a period of two years and making the appropriate calculations. And even then, questions would still remain as to whether weight should be given to blocking decisions (recognizing that making no decision may be construed as a decision not to act), whether the really important decisions should count as much as others, and so forth.

We make this point because in developing indicators for this study our methods required that we simplify reality and seek generalizations about conditions that have many subtle dimensions. To some extent we have sacrificed the in-depth detail of the case study approach to obtain the broader view of the population survey. There are, of course, benefits and disadvantages to both approaches. The case study is limited in the amount of social terrain that can be covered (at most usually a few cases), but it is substantial, because it puts the investigator closer to the reality of the phenomena. The survey approach tends to put the investigator further from the reality under examination but allows for comparative analysis of many cases.

The data used in this book were obtained by different methods from various sources: structured interviews with upper-echelon officials in the Department of Housing and Urban Development (HUD); a questionnaire survey of City Demonstration Agencies (CDAs); and content analysis of HUD documents and reports made on each city. Where it was necessary to transform qualitative judgments into quantitative form we attempted to obtain data on these judgments from at least two independent sources in order to increase confidence in our measures. Still, our indicators are, at best, approximations of the subtle and complex phenomena with which this study deals. How well our indicators reflect the reality we are seeking to comprehend is, ultimately, for the reader to decide.

SOURCES OF DATA

Interviews

Structured interviews were conducted with eleven HUD officials in Washington, D.C. (most of whom were known in the bureaucratic jargon as "deskmen") who were responsible for managing and maintaining relationships with city and regional staff; each of these officials had direct responsibility for Model Cities Programs in from twelve-to-thirty cities within a region; taken together these officials had covered all of the first-round and second-round programs over the planning year on into the first action year. At the time of the interviews, September, 1971, some of these officials had moved to other positions in HUD or to other programs.

Each interviewee was asked to make a comparative rating of the Model Cities Programs under their jurisdiction for seventeen variables including: degree of citizen influence; support of the chief executive; CDA director's accountability to MNA residents; and quality of the Comprehensive Development Plan. Most of the ratings were made along a five-point continuum ranging from "weakest" to "strongest," "least" to "most," and the like. To assist respondents in making these judgments and to allow for comparability of ratings, descriptions were provided of the behaviors and activities that characterized the two extremes and the midpoint on the continuum.

These interviews averaged two hours and both authors were present, except for a few cases where scheduling required that two respondents be interviewed at the same time. The officials that we interviewed gave both time and thought to the project. They expressed virtually no reservations in talking about the Model Cities Program experiences or in making comparative judgments about the programs under their jurisdictions. As some of the respondents indicated, this high degree of cooperation was due, in part, to the fact that, by the summer of 1971, federal interest in the Model Cities Program had diminished considerably; revenue sharing was on the horizon, and it appeared to HUD officials that the program would probably be phased out in the not-too-distant future. Also, by 1971 the Model Cities Program was no longer controversial. Thus, the respondents felt free to express their opinions. They seemed pleased to support an attempt to record their knowledge and their perspectives.

The reliability of the interview responses may be somewhat reduced by the fact that the respondents were asked about past events; there was no way to take account of their different abilities to recall accurately. This problem would not have arisen, of course, had the interviews been conducted at the time the events were taking place. On the other hand, because of the politically sensitive nature of many of the Model Cities experiences, it is likely that respondents would have been more reluctant to share their opinions and judgments at that time. Therefore, what we may have lost in reliability is probably compensated for by the fullness and openness of the responses.

While unable to insure the accuracy of respondents' recall, we were able to obtain additional data from narrative documents written on each program at the time the events took place. In several cases, these additional data were used as a second set of ratings and to test the reliability of responses. In some cases the second ratings were incorporated into the operational definitions of the study variables.

Documents

The major documentary sources drawn upon for analysis are narrative reports written by HUD regional staff, known as "leadmen." The leadmen were responsible for monitoring and providing various forms of assistance to the programs in their regions. As part of their monitoring activities these regional staff prepared "briefing memos" and quarterly reports on each program under their jurisdiction, which were forwarded to the deskmen at HUD in Washington, D.C. The briefing memos were summary reports written at the end of the planning year and the first action year. These documents described each program's experience in terms of progress made, obstacles encountered, and general program strengths and weaknesses. Three of the main subheadings of these reports referred to utilization of resources; administrative capability and local commitment; and community participation. For example, accounts of citizen participation in two programs were given as follows:

> The plan was basically developed by CDA and agency staff. The four Model Area Planning councils participated actively in the problem analysis but after that their role was primarily one of reacting to City proposals (Chicago).

> The City-citizen relationship can be characterized as a partnership in which the citizens have an active, initiating, strong role. The citizens have an important part to play; but it is still a partnership, completely dependent on active City support in formulating and implementing plans. Thus far, the partnership appears to be a success (Cambridge).

The quarterly reports are narrative records of program progress during the first action year, similar to the briefing memos, but prepared on a quarterly basis. Quarterly reports were used to obtain data in the cases where the briefing memos were not available, usually because these programs were funded in the second round (between November 1968 and early 1969) and had not completed their first action year at the time of the study.

A content analysis of these documents was done by three readers who independently rated each program for degree of citizen participation in planning, chief executive support, and implementation of citizen participation and coordination in the first action year. The ratings were made along a three-point continuum based on sets of descriptions of behaviors that characterized each point. (These descriptions of variables were the same as those used to elicit deskmen responses to the interview questions.) Ratings given these variables for each program were accepted if at least two readers were in agreement; otherwise the rating was discarded, and no score given that variable for the program on which agreement was not reached. This rating procedure was also used to analyze documents prepared by Interagency Review Committees involved in the selection of Model Cities Program participants. (The use of data on the selection process are described in detail in chapter 9.)

In addition to the above sources, information on each program's budget expenditures (for supplemental funds) in the first action year was provided by the HUD accounting office. Data on previous experience in urban renewal and public housing programs were obtained from the *Urban Renewal Directory, 1967* and the *Consolidated Development Directory, 1967.*

As described above, our information-gathering effort appears a systematic and straightforward process. However, as with many reports on social research, this is a cosmetic version of reality. The following anecdote may convey to the reader a sense of the obstacles and windfalls that sometimes underlie the smooth and powdered surface of rationality.

At the beginning of the study we visited the main HUD office building in Washington, D.C. for one week to conduct interviews with officials and to collect the necessary documents that HUD allowed us to borrow for analysis. We found some of the briefing memos and quarterly reports in the HUD library, but most were scattered in files around the various deskmen's offices in the building. We were given free access to these files and were able to obtain almost all of the documents we had come for. (In this process HUD officials went so far as to have more than ten cartons of data on Interagency Review Committee summaries for the Planning Grant Review Project retrieved from their storage warehouse in Maryland and delivered to us. This required two trips because the wrong cartons of material were retrieved on the first attempt.) By the end of the week we were missing approximately a dozen briefing memos.

In the process of interviewing and searching about the building we often passed the library, outside of which a wall of cartons (about one hundred, piled six feet high) stood waiting to be shipped to the warehouse for storage. When we first saw these cartons, one of the authors lightly suggested that we might spend a few hours investigating their contents. The thought of unloading and rummaging through one hundred cartons of material, however, was not appealing to the other author. While the initial suggestion was by-passed, it became more insistent as the week wore on. By the end of the week, with a dozen briefing memos still missing, the suggestion had turned into an exhortation about leaving no stone unturned, as well as a direct challenge in the form of a small wager concerning what one might expect to find in those cartons. The challenge was accepted. (The reluctant researcher's reservations about this undertaking were based not only on the dubious possibility of success. He felt that it might tarnish the dignified image of two Berkeley professors to be seen scrounging about amongst all those cartons and papers, blocking passage, and otherwise causing a small scene in the middle of the hallway of a national agency.) Nevertheless, we set about the work of lifting, unloading, and examining the contents of this wall of boxes. Somewhere around the ninety-fifth box the missing briefing memos were uncovered, at which point there was an exchange of cash accompanied by a sermon on the virtues of persistence in social research.

Surveys

To complete the study we needed a number of specific facts about the Model Cities Program that HUD either had not collected or had not organized for retrieval. The quickest and least expensive way to obtain these data was through a mail survey of all the programs. The U.S. Conference of Mayors, interested in some of the questions we wanted to ask, sponsored the project. From our viewpoint, their sponsorship of the survey was likely to insure a strong response rate. A questionnaire addressed to CDA directors was sent to the 147 programs, and the rate of return was 76 percent.

The questionnaire asked about: (1) the experience and educational background of CDA directors and staff; (2) size and ethnic composition of the Model Neighborhood Area (target neighborhood); (3) the structural relationships of resident organization staff to the CDA; (4) the roles of the CDA director and staff; (5) the number and kinds of public and private agencies participating in the program and the continuity of their participation from the planning year to the first action year; and (6) a breakdown of the CDA budget for the first action year in terms of the per cent of funds from supplemental, categorical, and other sources, and the agencies contributing funds.

Finally, a measure of turbulence-conflict for 1967–68 was obtained from data on a nationwide survey done by the Lemberg Center for the Study of Violence, Brandeis University, which the Center made available for our use.[2]

OPERATIONAL DEFINITIONS
OF INDICATORS

In chapter 2 we discussed a series of theoretical propositions on community planning which concerned phenomena such as degree of citizen participation, chief executive support, and levels of performance in program implementation; in that discussion we alluded to, but did not directly address, the problems of operational definitions. Now we leave the realm of theorizing and enter the realm of empirical measurement where the phenomena under consideration pose a number of methodological difficulties. Specifically, many of the indicators used in this study involve subjective ratings of units of analysis that are not very concrete; in some cases, a large inferential step is made between the empirical referent and the phenomenon it represents; and in some cases a combination of these conditions is present. We will explain these conditions and how they were handled so that the reader may judge the extent to which our indicators approximate the reality of community planning in Model Cities.

Subjective Ratings: Quantifying the Qualitative

In cases where the units of analysis were tenuous, most of the measures were developed from qualitative judgments that were quantified along an ordinal scale. These judgments were obtained by two methods previously described: content analysis of HUD documents prepared by regional staff (leadmen) and structured interviews with HUD officials in Washington, D.C. (deskmen). Thus, it is important to emphasize that these indicators represent a "federal perspective" on what was happening in the Model Cities Program. In many respects this perspective probably allows for as clear a view of the Model Cities Program nationwide as could be hoped. These informants were close enough to a number of programs for a long enough period of time to make informed comparative judgments (as compared, for example, to local CDA staff or citizen participants who knew only their own programs); yet they were removed enough from these programs to allow their judgments to be made with a reasonable degree of objectivity (again, as compared to local staff or citizen participants whose investments in their own programs might color their views).

In addition, it should be noted that the two sets of judgments derived from the federal perspective, strictly speaking, are not totally independent. Originally, the briefing memos were prepared by regional HUD staff (leadmen) as reports for consumption by the deskmen in Washington, D.C. Hence, the views of the Washington officials we interviewed were based, in part, on the information received in these reports as well as through their direct contact with the programs. We expected that these two sets of judgments would show a high degree of consistency.

Based on these judgments, seven major indicators were defined and constructed.

Citizen Influence in the Planning Process. In developing this indicator we asked HUD officials to rate each of the programs under their jurisdiction along a five-point continuum of citizen influence on decision making, as this influence appeared during the *last* quarter of the planning period. This time frame was chosen because it was during the last quarter of the planning year that decision making for the Comprehensive Development Plan concentrated on the actual program proposals for the first action year. Also, focusing on the last quarter allowed for the fact that citizen participation often varied over the planning year and accurate generalizations about the entire period would be more difficult to make than generalizations about a strategic quarter. Finally, we had access to other data that focused mainly on this last quarter that could be compared with the deskmen's ratings. As bases for making judgments, deskmen were given criteria for the two ends and the midpoint of the rating continuum:

Weak citizen influence (staff influence is the major determinant in decision making): MNA residents functioned primarily to "legitimize" the planning processes and products originated by the CDA staff. At this end of the continuum, residents play a residual role in decisions and generally rubber-stamp the decisions of CDA staff.

Moderate citizen influence (parity relationship between resident groups and CDA staff): MNA residents and CDA staff shared responsibility for key planning decisions. At this midpoint on the continuum, residents and staff could be characterized as "equal partners" in the planning enterprise.

Strong citizen influence (resident influence is the major determinant in decision making): MNA residents exerted preponderant influence in the planning process. At this end of the continuum, residents could be characterized as directors of the planning process.

A second set of ratings on the degree of citizen influence was obtained from the content analysis of briefing memos on the programs. Each program was rated along a three-point continuum, based upon the above criteria. The two sets of ratings (deskmen judgments and content analysis of briefing memos) were correlated and demonstrated a high degree of association (gamma .667).[a] The interview ratings were then collapsed into a three-point continuum (1, 2 = weak, 3 = moderate, and 4, 5 = strong) and were again correlated with the content analysis ratings and briefing memos. This time the degree of association between the two sets of judgments was very strong (gamma .769). We selected the collapsed interview ratings as our indicator of citizen influence in the planning process.

Chief Executive Support. A procedure similar to that described above was used to obtain measures of chief executive support. HUD officials were asked to rate the programs under their jurisdictions

[a]The meaning of gamma is reviewed on pp. 61–62.

along a five-point continuum. Rating criteria were discussed, and general descriptions of the two ends and the midpoint of the continuum were given:

Limited support: Executive's support was primarily "lip service"; little action was taken on the program's behalf without much prodding.

Moderate support: Executive was positively associated with the program to the extent that he could be called upon to act on the program's behalf and frequently produced the desired result.

Active support: Executive was clearly identified as the program's backer; he acted not only on request, but frequently took the initiative in interventions with HUD and local agencies.

Content analysis of the briefing memos produced a second set of ratings on chief executive support along a three-point continuum based upon the above criteria. Correlations between ratings from the interviews and the content analysis showed a moderate degree of association (gamma .470). The two sets of ratings were combined into an index that produced a strong degree of association when correlated independently with each set of ratings (gamma .939 and gamma .734). This index was used as our indicator of chief executive support.

MNA Conflict. The HUD officials interviewed were asked to rate the cities under their jurisdiction in terms of the degree of conflict that accompanied the development of the MNA citizen participation structure. *A low degree of conflict* was described as a situation in which there was virtually no contest for leadership and jurisdiction among residents in the development of the MNA citizen participation structure. *Moderate conflict* described communities in which there were genuine contests for leadership among individuals and groups in the MNA; elections held in these situations were lively, but did not provoke intense feelings. *High conflict* situations were characterized as those in which the struggle for leadership was heated and intense.

Sufficient information on this variable was not found in the briefing memos to allow for comparative ratings to be made through the content analysis. Therefore, the indicators of MNA conflict in the development of citizen participation structures were based exclusively on the interview ratings. However, we did have an indicator of community turbulence-conflict during the planning years (1967-68) that was based on data from a nationwide survey conducted by the Lemberg Center for the Study of Violence, Brandeis University. This second set of data was somewhat different from our indicator of MNA conflict. These data focused on reported incidents of disorder for entire cities rather than MNAs, and the disorders included more extreme forms of social conflict than were usually manifest in struggles for MNA leadership. Though the indicators of MNA conflict and community turbulence-conflict were not directly comparable, it was expected that there would be a measure of correspondence between the degree of turbulence-conflict in the larger community and that which emerged in the Model Cities target neighborhood. Correlation between these two indicators showed a strong degree of association (gamma .618), and in the absence of more comparable data against which to match the subjective interview ratings, this relationship gives us some confidence in the accuracy of the MNA conflict indicator.

Political Integration of MNA Leaders. For this indicator HUD officials were asked to rate each city under their jurisdiction in regard to the extent to which the leadership of MNA citizen participation structures were integrated into the administrative and political apparatus of city government. Raters made their judgments according to degree of political integration as reflected in the following descriptions:

> *Low degree of political integration:* MNA citizen participation leadership is not fully accepted and engaged by city government.

> *Moderate degree of political integration:* MNA citizen participation leadership is accepted by city government and engaged on an informal *ad hoc* basis when support and cooperation on specific projects are sought.

> *High degree of political integration:* MNA citizen participation leadership is engaged in formal ongoing communications and cooperation with city government.

Citizen Participation During the First Program Year. Ratings from the interviews and content analysis of first program year briefing memos and quarterly reports were incorporated in the development of this indicator. Citizen participation during the first program year was assessed in terms of the degree to which MNA residents were involved in, and able to influence, decisions concerning program review and evaluation, and ongoing planning efforts. The two sets of rating judgments were correlated and showed a substantial degree of association. The ratings were then combined into an index that was closely associated with each set of ratings. This index is our indicator of citizen participation during the first program year.

Quality of Agency Participation in Planning. This is a measure of quality of agency participation during the planning period. It was developed using the same operations as described for the preceding variables.

Coordination During the First Program Year. This indicator was developed using the same procedures as above. HUD officials were asked to rate programs according to the degree of interagency coordination achieved during the first program year. Here the operational measures of coordination refer to the extent to which Model Cities Programs were able to mesh complementary activities of federal, state, and local agencies through, for example, exchange of resources, joint planning, and joint decision-making procedures. A second set of coordination ratings was obtained through content analysis of federal reports. The two sets were correlated and showed a moderate degree of association. An index was constructed by combining the two sets of ratings. This produced a high degree of association when correlated independently with each set of ratings (gamma .965 and .612). This index represents our indicator of coordination during the program year.

Outcome Measures: Inferential Bases for Performance Indicators

As described in the study framework (chapter 2), the dynamics of community planning are analyzed in reference to outcome measures of: the planning process; the quality of the formal document that was produced (the Comprehensive Demonstration Plan); and the degree of success in program implementation. Seven performance indicators were selected to operationalize these outcomes.

Citizen Influence in the Planning Process. One of the major performance criteria used by HUD to evaluate the planning process was the extent to which local residents were involved as influential participants in decision making. As already noted in this regard, the planning process was perceived not only as a means, but also as an end valued in its own right. Thus, we treat citizen participation as both a characteristic of the action system and an outcome measure.[3] The "good" or "positive" outcome is measured by the extent to which residents controlled the course of events that would shape their communities, operationally defined by the indicator of citizen influence previously explained.

Quality of the Comprehensive Demonstration Plan. The planning year culminated in the development of a Comprehensive Demonstration Plan (CDP), which was submitted to HUD for approval prior to granting funds for the first program year. The quality of this plan was another dimension of performance upon which the Model Cities were judged. HUD's expectations for these plans were quite high. It was anticipated that CDPs would include innovative designs for the mobilization, concentration, and coordination of resources based upon clearly articulated rational analyses. Our interviews with HUD officials revealed that, while some CDPs were viewed as better than others, very few achieved this high level of expectation. In this study we have not sought to analyze the substantive details of the plans submitted by each city, most of which ran over hundreds of pages. Instead we selected three broad indicators by which to make some relative assessments of CDP quality.

The first indicator is self-explanatory. It is based on judgments of HUD officials who were asked to evaluate the general overall quality of the CDPs produced by cities under their jurisdictions. Interviewees were not asked to rate every city but, rather, to select those cities that produced the plans they considered "best" and those cities that produced the plans they considered "worst." In this manner, ratings were obtained on 105 CDPs, with positive impressions outweighing negative impressions approximately two to one.

The second indicator of CDP quality is based on the composition of the first program year budget that was included in the plan. The specific measures are the proportions of the total CDP budget that were represented by categorical funds and by local funds. The proportions of categorical funds anticipated in the budget is employed as an indicator of "quality" of the plan because it reflects a city's performance with regard to mobilization and concentration of resources. One of HUD's objectives in its methods of financing was to provide to the Model Cities a form of seed money, called "supplemental" funds, that would attract funding from other sources, primarily categorical monies. To the extent that a CDP demonstrated the city's ability to muster a large proportion of outside resources, or at least get them down on paper, we infer that it came closer to satisfying the concentration and mobilization of resources objectives than a CDP budget that was based on a small proportion of categorical funds. This is not meant to infer, however, that a city with a high proportion of categorical funds in its CDP budget was able to *imple-*

ment the concentration and mobilization of resources objectives more successfully than other cities when it came to putting programs into operation. Thus, while this indicator is used as a measure of "CDP quality" in line with HUD's standards, it should not be confused with measures of program implementation.

The percentage of local funds in the CDP budget is used as an indicator of a CDA's capacity to work with local executive government rather than with agencies. Our reasoning here is that local contributions were more likely to be reckoned as part of the overall city budget and, unlike categorical funds, were not dependent on the CDA's capacity to work successfully with specific agencies.

The third indicator of quality of the CDP is based on the number of agencies identified as having formal responsibility for carrying out projects proposed for the first program year. This indicator of "quality" again reflects one of HUD's performance standards: coordination. From the number of agencies with designated roles in the CDP we infer the "degree of coordination effort" that the plan proposed. This is not to imply that coordination during the program year would be implemented successfully; if anything it would probably be more difficult to achieve coordination because of the greater number of units involved. We award "quality" points to the CDPs that contained larger numbers of agencies on the assumption that these plans were more responsive to performance requirements set by HUD.

Success in Program Implementation. The ultimate test of a city's performance was its ability to implement plans and deliver services. Among other things, this involved spending the funds allocated for the program, which followed completion of the CDP and its approval by HUD. The indicators we selected to compare performance in this area are simple and straightforward: the percent of supplemental funds spent by each city at six months, at twelve months, and the per capita amount of supplemental funds spent at twelve months (the amount of supplemental funds spent divided by the MNA population). As it turned out, spending money (program implementation) was more difficult than many cities had anticipated. As of April 1971, only 23 percent of the sixty-five cities that had completed their first program year had been able to spend 50 percent or more of their supplemental budgets.

These indicators do not tap major substantive aspects of program implementation which might be measured along other dimensions. Who was served? What was the nature of the projects? How innovative, efficient, and effective were they? Which is to say that the indicators do not tell us how *well* the money was spent. While specific substantive measures of quality would have been useful, evaluating the overall success of implementation for a program with 10 percent of its projects in operation against the overall success of a program with 90 percent of its projects going would, ultimately, require giving some weight to the proportion of funds spent as an outcome measure. In any case, acquiring other evaluative measures of the success of program implementation would have entailed resources far in excess of those available for this study. However, we did obtain general qualitative judgments as seen from the perspective of HUD officials who were asked to designate those cities they considered "most successful" and "least successful" in implementing their programs. And there was substantial agreement between these qualitative judgments and the percent of supplemental funds spent for twelve months (gamma .459).

APPROACH TO DATA ANALYSIS

The relationships among variables in this study are described in two basic forms: by percentages in contingency tables, and by a statistical measure of association known as gamma. The objective of both methods is to summarize large bodies of data for ease of understanding and interpretation.

Percentages simplify descriptions of relationships among variables by equalizing the bases (to 100) upon which variable scores are calculated. This allows us to compare relative differences among the units being examined. Where percentages appear in contingency tables they have been calculated in the direction of the variable that is antecedent to the other variable or, if the time sequence between variables is indeterminate, in the direction of the variable that is considered to be the influencing factor in the relationship under examination.

Gamma is a measure of association between variables that form ordinal scales (ranked low-to-high, weak-to-strong), the form in which most of the data are presented. Gamma tells us the degree to which cities' ranks or ratings on one program variable are related to ranks or ratings on another. The relationships can go in two directions: toward perfect agreement among rankings (gamma +1.00) and toward perfect disagreement (gamma −1.00). Agreement indicates that a city ranking high on one variable also ranks high on the other. Disagreement indicates that a city ranking high on one variable ranks low on the other. It is extremely rare to obtain gamma correlations as high as +1.00 or −1.00 when dealing with phenomena as complex as relationships in community planning. Usually gammas of +.5 or −.5 are considered to represent substantial degrees of association. A concrete illustration of the general use and interpretation of gamma as shown in table 3-1 may dispel initial discomforts that some readers may feel when confronted with statistical measures in the abstract without specification of how they were computed.[4] In this table we describe the relationship between the degree of citizen influence in planning and four other variables in order to illustrate some of the different values of gamma.

As shown, in table 3.1 there is substantial agreement (or positive association) between the degree of conflict in the Model Neighborhood Area (MNA) and the degree of citizen influence in the planning process (gamma .644). This means that the *higher* its rank in MNA conflict, the more likely a program was to have *strong* citizen influence in the planning process. Or conversely, the *lower* a program ranks in terms of MNA conflict, the more likely it is to have developed *weak* citizen influence. (Technically, the gamma here of .644 indicates that there is a 64.4 percent greater agreement than disagreement between all program ranks on both these variables.) The degree of resident control over resident organization staff has only a low-positive association with degree of citizen influence in planning (gamma .283). Thus, programs in which residents had a high degree of control over resident organization staff are more likely to have strong citizen influence. The low negative correlation between the degree of citizen influence and the number of agencies that played an active role in the planning period (gamma −.154) suggests that programs with *higher* numbers of agencies active in the planning process were a little more likely to have had *lower* degrees of citizen influence than programs that engaged smaller numbers of agencies during

Table 3-1. Relationships Between Selected Variables and Degree of Citizen Influence in the Planning Process[a]

Variables	Gamma	Strength of Correlation
Degree of Conflict in Model Neighborhood Area	.644	Substantial-Positive
Resident Control over Staffing Arrangements of Resident-Organizations	.283	Low-Positive
Number of Agencies with an Active Role in the Planning Period	−.154	Low-Negative
Chief Executive Support	.064	Negligible-Positive

[a]The conventions used for describing the value of gamma are recommended by Davis.[5]

planning. Finally, the negligible correlation between citizen influence and chief executive support (gamma .064) indicates that there is no discernible linear relationship between these variables; that is, there was almost as much agreement in rankings (high, high) as disagreement (high, low). Because the gamma coefficients reflect the general tendency toward linear relationships, a very low gamma value does not eliminate the possibility that a curvilinear relationship (in the form of a parabola) exists among the variables. And in a few cases where low correlations are obtained, a nonlinear relationship appears when the data are examined in contingency tables. These cases will be identified in our analysis.

NOTES

1. Émile, Durkheim, *The Division of Labor in Society*, trans. by George Simpson (New York: Free Press Edition, 1964), pp. 424-26.

2. For a description of Lemberg Center survey, see Jane Baskin et al., *Race Relations, Civil Disorders 1967-1969* (Report No. 1, Lemberg Center for the Study of Violence, Waltham, Mass.: Brandeis University, 1971).

3. For a stimulating view of the planning process as an end, see John Friedmann, *Retracking America* (New York: Anchor-Doubleday, 1973).

4. The computations for this study were done through the use of the Berkeley Transposed File Statistical System, a computer program (otherwise known as PICKLE). The technical details on computation of ordinal measures of association may be found in a number of basic texts and articles. For example, see James A. Davis, *Elementary Survey Analysis* (Englewood Cliffs, N.J.: Prentice-Hall, Inc., 1971); Linton C. Freeman, *Elementary Applied Statistics* (New York: John Wiley and Sons, Inc., 1968); and Leo Goodman and William Kruskal, "Measures of Association for Cross Classification," *Journal of the American Statistical Association* 49 (1954): 732-64.

5. Davis, p. 49.

✳ Part II

Community Planning System

✳ Chapter 4

The Action System

The policy issue that received popular attention in the 1960s concerned the appropriate roles and relationships of local citizen organizations, professionals, and political leaders in community planning agencies. While the objectives of "community participation" were hotly debated, there was little consensus on the precise meanings of these terms. Interpretations often varied according to personal inclinations and political perspectives. For example, two major critiques of the war on poverty, one by Kenneth Clark and the other by Daniel Patrick Moynihan, expressed dissatisfaction with the implementation of these objectives in the Economic Opportunity Program. Clark said that there was too little citizen participation and Moynihan that there was too much.[1] Similarly, both the Democrats and the Republicans levelled charges of inadequate citizen participation and developed legislation to correct matters, each party carrying forward quite different objectives under the same populist banner. "Citizen participation" and "community control" are the kinds of slogans that can be made to fit a wide range of specific programmatic and political objectives; hardly anyone can disagree that citizens should participate and that communities should control, because collectivities of any size or shape or color can be called "communities," and "participation" can take many forms ranging from passive observation to active assertive direction.[2] Thus, it is no surprise to find the Republican revenue sharing program, which enhanced the participation and control of mayors and governors, justified with the same rhetoric about "local control" as was used for the Economic Opportunity Program, which was to have increased the participation and control of the poor.

In the Model Cities Program a good deal of the planning effort addressed questions of the appropriate relationships between residents and CDA staff in the planning process. At the conclusion of the Model Cities planning "year" (which in fact lasted anywhere from ten months to two years for different cities), the City Demonstration Agencies (CDAs) submitted a Comprehensive Demonstration Plan (CDP) to the Department of Housing and Urban Development (HUD). Much of the work of the CDA during this planning period was devoted to creating an action system able to produce this plan, a system within which information could be gathered and exchanged, and decisions could be agreed upon by parties relevant to the Model Cities Program. By statute, that system was required to be composed of local residents as well as the CDA staff. However, cities varied considerably in regard to the ways in which these elements were combined. The arrangements varied in terms of the number and size of policy-making groups, authority structures, communications systems, decision-making and allocation systems, and degrees of input from citizens and experts.[3]

In examining the action system, our primary attention will be given to the decision-making relationships that developed between citizen organizations and CDA staff, specifically the degrees of influence exercised by these two major parties to the community planning enterprise. As chapter 3 showed, the patterns of influence reflecting these decision-making relationships were operationally defined and ordered as follows:

1. *Staff Dominance:* MNA residents exercise negligible influence on decision making, functioning mainly to rubber-stamp staff decisions.
2. *Parity:* MNA residents and staff share responsibility for key planning decisions.
3. *Resident Dominance:* MNA residents exert preponderant influence on decision making.

In this chapter, the first part of our analysis of the action system, the patterns of influence are analyzed to determine how the following are associated with different types of action systems: demographic features of the MNA; structural arrangements for participation; sociopolitical conditions; and professional backgrounds and roles of CDA personnel. The purpose here is to determine the extent to which characteristics of the action system are associated with the emergence of different patterns of influence. In the second part of the action system analysis, chapter 5, we consider the extent to which variations in patterns of influence and other characteristics of the action system are associated with different outcomes of product and performance.

Before examining how different characteristics of the action system are related to patterns of influence, let us offer a few observations on the overall distribution of patterns of influence found among the 142 cities for which ratings were obtained. First, as shown in Table 4-1, over 50 percent of the cities failed to achieve more than a negligible degree of citizen influence in the planning process, while less than 20 percent developed systems in which citizen influence was a determining force. As noted earlier, the weighting of this distribution against the achievement of strong citizen influence is generally reflected in the literature on citizen participation during the 1960s in a variety of program areas. On the other hand, in 44 percent of the cases there was at least a moderate degree of citizen influence. Given the fragmented data available, broad comparisons with other program areas are necessarily tenuous. However, we tentatively venture the judgment that citizen influence in community planning probably was not on the whole substantially greater or less in Model Cities than in other programs of the 1960s. It is also interesting to note that there was virtually no difference in the distribution of patterns of influence in the planning period between first-round and second-round funded cities. Fifty-six percent of first-round cities were classified as having staff-dominant patterns of influence compared to 55 percent of second-round cities.

These data, therefore, do not reflect the shift in HUD policy on citizen participation that occurred when the Nixon administration took office. As it developed, the Nixon administration's urban strategy was intended to strengthen the regular institutional channels of local government, which meant reducing the power (or potential for

Table 4-1.   Round Funded and Patterns of Influence

Patterns of Influence	Round Funded		
	1st Round (percent)	2nd Round (percent)	Total (percent)
Staff Dominant	56	55	56
Parity	23	29	26
Resident Dominant	21	16	18
Total	100	100	100
	(n=73)	(n=69)	(142)

power) of independent citizen organizations that operated outside of this institutional structure. The reason table 4-1 does not reflect this policy is that the second-round cities were selected and funded for planning during the Johnson administration (end of 1968). The major *formal* indications of the change in emphasis concerning citizen participation, which superseded the earlier HUD guidelines, were contained in CDA Letters 10A and 10B, dated December 1969 and March 1970, respectively.[4] That is, the change in policy was introduced at the end of the planning period for second-round cities.

CHARACTERISTICS OF THE ACTION SYSTEM

There seems to have been general agreement within HUD that citizen influence in the planning process was desirable, but opinions differed on precisely how much. Did it mean citizen control over the program, or at least the power of veto, or perhaps the type of normative influence that partners might exercise over each other? Though HUD staff held varying views on these questions, the differences ranged mostly in the area between parity and resident-dominant patterns of influence. Planning processes in which CDA staff dominated decision making and resident participants served merely a rubber-stamp function were the least consistent with the general guidelines set forth in HUD's planning model (as well as with conceptions of the management personnel we interviewed at HUD). Yet, the staff-dominant pattern of influence appeared in over half the cities.

What characteristics of action systems distinguished those in which citizen influence developed in different degrees? There are various findings and assertions concerning this question in the literature on community planning, some of which were reviewed in chapter 2. In the following analysis the relationships between patterns of influence and demographic, sociopolitical, organizational, and staff characteristics of the action system, illustrated in figure 4-1, will be explored.

Demographic Characteristics of the MNA: Size and Racial Composition

MNA Size.   Yin et al. found that in a sample of fifty-one social-welfare-related programs strong citizen influence was more likely to emerge in small target areas (less than 20,000) than in large target areas (over 20,000).[5] These findings, however, are not supported by the experiences of citizen participation in Model Cities. On the contrary, using the same operational definitions of small and large target

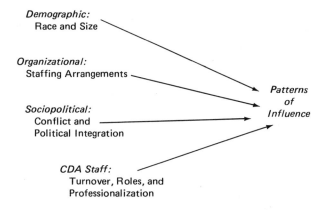

Figure 4-1. Action System Characteristics and Patterns of Influence

areas, we found a moderate-positive relationship (gamma .309) between MNA size and the strength of citizen influence, as shown in table 4-2.

Different theoretical explanations can be offered to support findings of either a positive or a negative relationship between target area size and patterns of citizen influence. For example, the explanation of an inverse relationship might be that in small target areas there are fewer fragmented groups and more possibilities for communication with the whole, thereby making it easier to weld a cohesive majority that can present a strong united front in dealing with city agencies such as CDAs. On the other hand, in community planning as in other political endeavors there is strength in sheer numbers which might explain findings of a positive relationship between area size and patterns of influence. On the general relationship between the size of an urban district and its capacity to exercise influence on city agencies, Jacobs observes:

Table 4-2. Model Neighborhood Area Size and Patterns of Influence

| | MNA Size | |
| | Under 20,000 | Over 20,000 |
Patterns of Influence	*(percent)*	*(percent)*
Staff Dominant	67	49
Parity	22	33
Resident Dominant	12	18
Total	101[a]	100
	(n=69)	(n=39)
(gamma .309)		

[a] due to rounding

How big, in absolute terms, must an effective district be? I have given a functional definition of size: big enough to fight city hall, but not so big that street neighborhoods are unable to draw district attention and to count.

In absolute terms, this means different sizes in different cities, depending partly on the size of the city as a whole. In Boston, the North End had a population upward of 30,000 people when it was strong in district power. Now its population is about half that. . . . Cohesive though the North End is, it has lost an important sum of district power. In a city like Boston, Pittsburgh, or possibly even Philadelphia, as few as 30,000 people may be sufficient to form a district. In New York or Chicago, however, a district as small as 30,000 amounts to nothing. On the maximum side, I know of no district larger than 200,000 which operates like a district.[6]

During the planning period for Model Cities the size of most target areas was approximately proportionate to the size of the cities in which they were located. According to HUD guidelines the population of MNAs was limited to 10 percent of the total population in large cities and a higher percent in small cities. If it is true, as Jacobs observes, that proportionate not so much as absolute strength in numbers is required for an urban district to exercise influence on city agencies, then the MNAs could be considered fairly equal in strength. This is not reflected in our findings, which indicate a positive correlation between MNA size and citizen influence. Thus, the proportionate relationship between MNA size and city size in the Model Cities population weakens the plausibility of the "strength in numbers" explanation for our findings. At the same time, however, because city size and MNA size are so closely associated on a rank order basis, it is possible that there is something about the more inclusive unit of city size, rather than MNA size, that might account for the different patterns of influence that emerged. This line of analysis is pursued in chapter 7 where we examine the extent to which contextual factors such as city size are associated with patterns of influence and we discuss relevant theories concerning these types of relationships.

Racial Composition. There is disagreement in the community planning literature regarding the manner in which the proportion of minority residents in target areas is related to the amount of influence and control obtained through citizen participation. One view, for which there is empirical evidence, suggests that citizen influence varies directly with the proportion of minority residents in the target area (pp. 33–34). The opposing view, for which there is also empirical evidence, suggests that racial homogeneity in the target area has no bearing on citizen influence (see p. 34). Generally, the popular impression is that citizen influence is quite forceful in neighborhoods composed predominantly of minority residents. This popular view has been amplified by Wolfe's description of "mau-mauing the flak catchers."[7] It is possible that these discrepancies reflect the limited sizes and nonrepresentative nature of the program samples in the studies cited. In any event, additional evidence from the Model Cities experience may help clarify the issue.

As indicated in table 4-3, the racial composition of MNAs had no direct relationship to the degree of citizen influence in the Model Cities program (gamma .026). Resident-dominant patterns of influence appeared in 16 percent of the MNAs with relatively small percentages of minority residents and in 14 percent of the MNAs with both medium and large percentages of minority residents, And staff-dominant patterns of influence developed in well over half the programs where minority residents were either a small proportion (39 percent or less) or a large proportion (over 75 percent) of the MNA population.

These findings run counter to the popular impression that in communities where they constitute a majority of the population, racial minorities exert greater influence over local programs than residents in other communities. Among the factors that contributed to this popular view (other than the empirical evidence, which is somewhat divided on the issue) were the urban riots of the sixties; these events created the image of minorities controlling, or being well on their way to controlling, their neighborhoods. The news media gave much attention to the extremist, assertive, and nationalistic elements among minority communities; controversial efforts to achieve community control of local public schools in minority neighborhoods in New York City made national headlines; the Black Panthers of Oakland, California, and their goals of community control also achieved

Table 4-3. Percent of Racial Minorities in the Model Neighborhood Area and Patterns of Influence

Patterns of Influence	Percent Minority in MNA		
	Low (39 or less)	*Medium (40–74)*	*High (75 or more)*
Staff Dominant	72	47	63
Parity	12	39	23
Resident Dominant	16	14	14
Total	100	100	100
	(n=25)	(n=36)	(n=43)
(gamma .026)			

national prominence. The tactics of confrontation were employed widely in community action programs.[8] Overall, there was considerable ferment in minority communities with declared objectives of community control, at least by the most vocal elements in these communities. With the tactics of confrontation lively, and the calls for community control loud, it is not difficult to get the impression that to some degree the haled event became a reality. We think that, in part, the popular impression of strong minority influence on programs in their communities stems not from a careful analysis of the results of planning (how often they actually gained enough power to be influential) but rather from the considerable attention given to the confrontation process. This is not to argue that these activities had no effect on resident influence in minority neighborhoods, but rather that the increase in influence that occurred was somewhat less than that conveyed in public images.

There is another reason why citizen influence should generally seem strong in communities with a high proportion of racial minority residents. Historically, in communities where religious and ethnic minorities were in the majority, these groups achieved a high degree of political influence and control over their neighborhoods. And up to the present there is still much evidence that communities with populations composed of large proportions of religious and ethnic minorities tend to exhibit high degrees of political competition.[9] However, Lineberry and Fowler, in a study of two hundred American cities, found that this relationship does not appear to hold for nonwhite minorities, although it did for religious and ethnic groups.[10] Thus, confrontations and rhetoric notwithstanding, it seems that nonwhite communities have not yet achieved the political and social power of religious and ethnic minorities. Our findings would lend some support to this view. At the very least, these findings would lead us to reject notions that the racial minority residents of the target areas will always have substantial impact on the patterns of citizen influence that develop in community planning.

Sociopolitical Characteristics of the MNA: Conflict and Political Integration

Conflict. The requirements for citizen participation held forth an opportunity for individuals and groups within the MNAs to achieve positions of relative influence and to reap some of the benefits that typically accrue to such positions. But since all MNA residents and groups obviously could not share equally in these benefits, competition to control the resident organization in the MNA developed to varying degrees in different Model Cities as the organizational structure for citizen participation took shape. In approximately half of the Model Cities there was a low degree of conflict, with little competition for leadership in the development of the MNA citizen participation structure. The remaining cities were split almost evenly between those in which there was a moderate degree of conflict, with lively elections and real contests for leadership, and those in which there was a high degree of conflict, with pronounced struggles for leadership clearly visible and felt in the development of the citizen participation structure.

As indicated in table 4-4, there is a strong relationship (gamma .664) between the degree of conflict within the MNA and the patterns of influence that emerged in different programs. In other words, where the degree of conflict in the development of citizen organizations was higher, there was greater likelihood of strong citizen influence in the planning system. This relationship might be explained in two ways. On the one hand, programs in which residents had major decision-making powers provided greater incentives to compete for leadership positions than programs in which staff control of decision making was established at the outset. On the other hand, cities in which there were high degrees of conflict in the MNA were more likely to have militant resident organizations than cities in which little conflict accompanied the development of the citizen participation structure. Moreover, the types of resident organizations forged through conflict would be strongly inclined to, and capable of, struggle with CDA staff for an influential role in Model Cities decision making. There is also some evidence that the degree of conflict in the MNA was associated with the degree of turbulence and violence in the city as a whole (p. 56). This association between MNA conflict and citywide turbulence suggests that it is more likely that conflict causes citizen dominance than the other way around. However,

Table 4-4. Model Neighborhood Area Conflict and Patterns of Influence

Patterns of Influence	Low (percent)	Medium (percent)	High (percent)
Staff Dominant	73	57	21
Parity	24	27	32
Resident Dominant	3	17	47
Total	100	101[a]	100
	(n=66)	(n=30)	(n=34)
(gamma .644)			

[a] due to rounding

it is difficult to distinguish which of these factors was the precipitating one with a high degree of assurance because of their almost concurrent development.

Political Integration. A second major characteristic of the sociopolitical environment of the action system is the degree to which MNAs were politically integrated with city government. While conflict in the MNA reflects the quality of turbulence and instability in the environment, political integration reflects elements of stability in the established lines of communication and working relationships between the MNA and the formal political apparatus of the city. The estimated degrees of political integration in the MNAs is based on the federal administrators' judgments of the extent to which citizen participation leadership of the MNA was accepted and systematically called upon to serve and work in concert with city government. As illustrated in table 4-5, there is a moderate-positive correlation (gamma .426) between political integration and patterns of influence. But an examination of these data reveals that this relationship differs from the relationship between conflict and patterns of influence in an important way. Whereas a high degree of conflict was most likely to occur along with a resident-dominant pattern of influence, high political integration occurred most frequently when decision-making influence was shared between CDA staff and residents in a parity arrangement.

By combining these two characteristics (conflict and political integration) it is possible to analyze the extent to which there are distinctive sociopolitical environments associated with the emergence of different patterns of influence. The results of this analysis (table 4-6) reveal that, indeed, three fairly well bounded sociopolitical environments can be identified in which each pattern of influence

Table 4-5. Political Integration of Model Neighborhood Area Leadership and Patterns of Influence

| | Political Integration of MNA Leadership | | |
Patterns of Influence	Low (percent)	Medium (percent)	High (percent)
Staff Dominant	73	56	21
Parity	12	23	62
Resident Dominant	15	21	17
Total	100	100	100
	(n=59)	(n=43)	(n=29)
(gamma .426)			

Table 4-6. Patterns of Influence and Sociopolitical Environment

| Degree of Conflict | A. Cities with Staff-Dominant Patterns of Influence | | | B. Cities with Parity Patterns of Influence | | | C. Cities with Resident-Dominant Patterns of Influence | | |
| | Degree of Political Integration (percent) | | | Degree of Political Integration (percent) | | | Degree of Political Integration (percent) | | |
	Low	Medium	High	Low	Medium	High	Low	Medium	High
Low	44	15	8	9	12	27	5	5	0
Medium	9	17	0	3	9	12	10	5	5
High	3	3	2	9	9	12	29	33	10
Total	101[a]			102[a]			102[a]		
	(n=66)			(n=34)			(n=21)		

[a]Due to rounding

occurs with the greatest frequency. Thus, at one end of the citizen influence continuum *cities in which there are staff-dominant patterns of influence are most likely to have sociopolitical environments characterized by low degrees of political integration and low degrees of conflict.* Forty-four percent of all staff-dominant cities are in this category, and another 41 percent are on its border. At the other extreme, *sociopolitical environments in the cities with resident-dominant patterns of influence are most likely to be characterized by high degrees of conflict and low-to-moderate degrees of political integration.* Sixty-two percent of all resident-dominant cities are in this category and another 15 percent are on its border. And finally, *parity patterns are found most frequently in cities with sociopolitical environments characterized by high degrees of political integration and low degrees of conflict.* Twenty-seven percent of all cities with parity-type patterns of influence fall into this category, with an additional 33 percent found in neighboring cells.

A theoretical explanation of these findings suggests that where there were low degrees of conflict in the development of the citizen participation structure, two possible conditions might have existed within the MNA. First, where residents and resident groups were unassertive, poorly organized, and in general politically inactive, there was little conflict. This was so because there was no initial organizational structures to serve as a vehicle for the expression of competing interests, and the political ambitions and skills to create such a vehicle were neither available in the necessary mass nor cultivated through technical assistance. In this case, we would anticipate low degrees of political integration merely because there is no viable local structure with which the city's political apparatus can be linked. These circumstances describe a sociopolitical environment that is highly conducive to the development of staff-dominant patterns of influence. The second case for limited conflict involves MNAs in which strong, well-recognized citizen organizations were in existence prior to the onset of Model Cities. Here internal conflicts had already been resolved or at least mitigated and MNA leaders were able to keep constituents under control. In this case we would anticipate moderate-to-high degrees of political integration because once a stable citizen organization has been built its leaders often may seek to enhance their legitimacy and power by establishing formal relationships with city hall. Moreover, efforts by the city's political apparatus to co-opt such citizen organizations are frequent and represent a good deal of what urban politics is all about. This sociopolitical environment provides fertile ground for the development of parity patterns of influence (table 4.6B).

According to this interpretation of the findings, the one combination of political integration and conflict that we would have expected to occur least frequently is the sociopolitical environment in which *both* conflict and political integration are high. The reason for this, in line with the explanation of the above cases, is that MNA leaders and organizations achieve integration into the city's political apparatus, at least in part, by exhibiting their capacity to maintain a degree of control and insure some stability over the organizational activities within the MNA. At the same time, political integration tends to reinforce stabilization within the MNA by enhancing the legitimacy of these leaders and organizations and making the formal political system readily available to them for mediating differences and dissatisfactions that might arise in the MNA. Hence, the prospects for intense conflict to be found in environments with high degrees of political integration would seem quite limited. In all, only seven cities fell into this category (table 4.6).

Organizational Characteristics: Staffing Arrangements for Citizen Participation Structure

In the community planning literature, staffing links between the official planning agencies such as CDAs, Community Action Agencies, and Urban Renewal Agencies and citizen participation structures are considered important factors associated with the development of citizen influence. Professional opinion and empirical evidence support the notion that when resident organizations have control over hiring of their own staff who are free to operate independently of the official planning agency, strong citizen influence is more likely to develop than when staff are assigned to the resident organization at the discretion of the planning agency.[11] During the early years of the Model Cities Program, HUD encouraged cities to provide independent technical assistance to citizen organizations. The rationale for this arrangement was expressed by Assistant Secretary Taylor:

The neighborhood structure must have the assistance it needs to bargain and negotiate effectively. This does not mean that it must do the planning, or that it must have a duplicate planning and staff capability.

It does mean making available technical assistance and expertise that the neighborhood can trust. With this assistance they can analyze, criticize, and suggest alternatives to be explored and developed, and judge whether the exploration of those alternatives has been honest and thorough.

The objective of the Model Cities program is to help develop the capacity to function in and use the system. Technical assistance is an indispensible tool. And if it is to be accepted, it must be trusted. In many places, to

be trusted it must be under the direction and control of the community.
That is why we are moving to encourage the concept of Independent
Technical Assistance—making available to the residents, under their con-
trol, resources to provide technical assistance and expertise they trust.[12]

Examining the experiences in Model Cities, we were able to identify the staffing pattern of citizen organizations in ninety-eight cities
in the planning period in terms of the following arrangements:

1. in forty-five cities the CDA hired and assigned staff that worked
   with residents' organizations;
2. in twenty-five cities the CDA hired and assigned staff that worked
   with residents based on recommendations of the residents'
   organization;
3. in twenty-five cities the residents' organization hired its own staff;
   and
4. in three cities the staffing of the residents' organization was con-
   tracted out to another agency.

Omitting the last arrangement, for which there are only three
cases, the first three staffing arrangements can be viewed as a scale of
resident control over their own staff. The relationship between the
degree of resident control over staff and patterns of influence is
presented in table 4-7.

As shown in table 4-7, the experience of Model Cities generally
sustains the proposition that resident control over staff of the citizen
participation structure is directly related to the ability of the citizen
organization to influence decision making, although the strength of
this relationship (gamma .283) is not as great as a reading of the
literature might suggest. While the data imply that citizen control
over staff increases the chances of achieving strong citizen influence
in decision making, this result is far from guaranteed. In slightly less

Table 4-7. Patterns of Influence and Resident Control Over Staff

	Resident Control Over Staff		
Patterns of Influence	*Staff hired by CDA and assigned to resident organization (percent)*	*Staff hired by CDA based on recommen- dations of resident organization (percent)*	*Staff hired by resident organization (percent)*
Staff Dominant	66.7	64	44
Parity	22.2	28	28
Resident Dominant	11.1	8	28
Total	100	100	100
	(n=45)	(n=25)	(n=25)
(gamma .283)			

than half (44 percent) of the cities in which residents hired their own staff, the citizen organizations were nevertheless unable to achieve even moderate degrees of influence.

An interpretation of this relationship should be made with the understanding that cause and effect (in the sense of which variable preceded the other in time) are unclear. Thus, it is possible that in cities in which resident influence was dominant, the right to hire their own staff may have been won by residents; or in cities in which residents hired their own staff, these staff may have provided the impetus for the development of resident-dominant patterns of influence.

CDA Staff Characteristics: Turnover, Roles, and Professionalization

In examining CDA staff characteristics we are concerned mainly with those of the CDA director, whose position between the elected officials and the staff and residents was central to the Model Cities planning process. The administrator's behavior in the case of Model Cities is, of course, not easily generalizable to all other organizations. Model Cities was a new program and, in many cities, it was mounted in the midst of great controversy. The goals of the program were defined only generally and vaguely by HUD; to those goals each of the cities added its own set of objectives, which frequently were just as general and vague. Upon assuming the job, the CDA director was faced with the task of creating an organizational system to do comprehensive social-physical planning for which there was little precedent. Thus, the CDA director held a pivotal position; he had to cope with all the demands and strains of operating from an executive position in what was usually a turbulent environment.

The CDA directors came to their positions from diverse backgrounds, and their responses to its opportunities and demands were varied. In analyzing how this element of the action system relates to the patterns of influence that developed in the planning period, we will focus upon the following questions: What types of roles did they emphasize during the planning and implementation phases of the program? How did the degree of professionalization of CDA staffs affect the director's authority? And, in general, how did the directors manage? Addressing the last issue in its most fundamental sense, we found that a substantial proportion of the CDA directors did not manage to hold their positions very long. The turnover rate for CDA directors clearly reflects the high-risk nature of this position.

Turnover of CDA Directors. In the period of time covered by the planning phase and the first program year (which ranged from two years to over-three years), approximately 46 percent of the cities had more than one CDA director. (This is a conservative estimate because at the time our data were gathered some of the cities had not yet completed their first program year.) A large proportion of this turnover took place in the period of transition from planning to first program year. defined as the period running from three-months-before to three-months-after the commencement of the first program year. Thirty-one percent, or almost one-third, of all the turnover occurred during this period. Thus, it appears that the change from planning to program implementation was a critical period in determining the CDA director's tenure.

A comparison of turnover rates in cities with different patterns of influence reveals that while these rates were fairly high across the board, they tended to increase slightly as the degree of citizen influence in the planning process increased. As shown in table 4-8, resident-dominant cities had an overall turnover rate 10 percent higher than staff-dominant cities, with the turnover rate for parity cities falling in the middle.

Though overall turnover rates for cities with different patterns of influence did not vary by more than 10 percent, turnover *during the transition period* was marked by a much wider range of variation. That is, CDA directors in parity cities experienced only 15 percent turnover in the transition period compared to turnover rates of 34 percent and 48 percent for staff-dominant and resident-dominant cities, respectively. Aside from knowing that turnover was low for parity cities in the transition period, we cannot otherwise pinpoint just when turnover did take place in each type of city, nor can we say just why this pattern occurred. One tentative interpretation might be that: (1) it was possible for planning, in the sense of devel-

Table 4-8.   Patterns of Influence and Turnover of CDA Directors

	Patterns of Influence		
	Staff-Dominant (percent)	Parity (percent)	Resident-Dominant (percent)
Total Turnover (CDAs with two or more directors during planning period and first program year)	43 (n=65)	48 (n=27)	53 (n=13)
Transition Turnover (Director left in period three months before to three months after beginning of first-year program)	34 (n=64)	15 (n=26)	48 (n=15)

oping a CDP, to be accomplished with limited involvement and weak support of various elements in the interorganizational field, such as the mayor's office; (2) but program implementation required a higher degree of good-will and cooperation with local agencies and city government (as we shall see in chapter 6, chief executive support and program implementation were strongly correlated); (3) parity cities, as noted earlier, tended to be characterized by higher degrees of political integration than staff-dominant and resident-dominant cities; (4) therefore, in parity cities, CDA directors, who were the connecting links between local agencies, city hall, and resident groups, experienced less strain in developing and cementing these necessary relationships as they entered the implementation phase than directors in staff-dominant and resident-dominant cities. There is partial support for the explanation that the degree of political integration was a factor in mitigating strains that developed during the transition period. As illustrated in table 4-9, an examination of the relationship between patterns of citizen influence and transition-period turnover, controlling for political integration, reveals that the lowest proportions of transition period turnover occurred where political integration was highest, regardless of the pattern of influence.

Process vs. Task in Social Planning

Should social planners pay more attention to process than to task? Should they devote their energies primarily to the cultivation of cooperative working relationships that will assure the social and political development of participants in the planning process? Or should they give foremost concern to achievement of delimited objectives such as completing a needs/resources survey, producing a master plan, and designing program components that will show tangible results?

These questions achieved central importance in the planning profession in the 1960s. Up until that period, professional planners had dealt with the city as a physical and economic enterprise; therefore,

Table 4-9. **Percent of Transition-Period Turnover by Political Integration and Patterns of Influence**

Percent of Transition Turnover by Patterns of Influence	Percent of Transition-Period Turnover by Degrees of Political Integration (PI)			
	Low PI	Medium PI	High PI	Total
Staff Dominant	65	20	15	100 (n=20)
Parity	50	25	25	100 (n=4)
Resident Dominant	33	50	17	100 (n=6)

they were largely concerned with questions of traffic management, business development, and housing as these factors affected the planner's objective of developing the city as an organism that could be dealt with rationally without the annoying intrusions of differences based upon social class, race, ethnicity, and inequality. However, the task-process debate in *social* planning had been carried on in a lively fashion for several decades in the fields of social work and social welfare.[13]

In the early 1960s the conceptual issues in the practice of community organization-social planning shifted from normative descriptions of "what it is" (interest in whether the task or process orientation is most central to the definition of practice) to analyses of "how to do it" (interest in when and where task or process is most useful). Both task and process had achieved roughly equal footing in accepted definitions of the professional social work practice of social planning-community organization.[14] With that development, the focus of practice concerns shifted to empirical questions about the conditions of professional practice under which either task or process orientations might be most effective. Our discussion here is addressed specifically to empirical questions about the degree to which task and process orientations at different stages of the social planning enterprise are associated with different outcomes. In dealing with these questions we examine the role orientations of the directors of City Demonstration Agencies (CDAs) and their relationships to a series of outcome variables. Before presenting the findings, a few words about the definition of process and task orientations are in order.

Dimensions of Process and Task. "Process" and "task" are conceptual labels used to distinguish both different professional roles and different goals of practice. While the ideas that these concepts seek to capture are meaningful, the labels are rather awkward, because in common usage it is difficult to imagine a practitioner performing any "task" without engaging in some sort of "process" or "a series of actions definitely conducing to an end." And in technical usage, as Rothman points out, "process goals may contain concrete task or substantive aspects."[15]

There are at least three dimensions of task and process orientations to practice suggested in the literature: *goals, degree of directiveness in behavior,* and *primary skills.*

As a *goal of practice,* process involves facilitating social relationships and enhancing capabilities; in comparison, task refers to achievement of more delimited and concrete outcomes associated with program development and social reform.

Two role dimensions of task and process can be distinguished. The first is the *degree of directiveness* exercised by the practitioner. Specifically, the process orientation has often been linked with *non-directive* role behavior and the task orientation with *directive* role behavior. Rothman's cogent analysis of this role dimension questions the necessary congruence of these relationships. He argues that, hypothetically, it is possible to conceive of either directive or non-directive behavior being applied in the pursuit of either task or process objectives.[16] While we would agree with Rothman's analysis of the theoretical possibilities, it does not necessarily follow that because something is possible in theory that it occurs in the real world. Rather, we think that the close association of nondirective behavior with process objectives and directive behavior with task objectives that is found in much of the community organization-social planning literature may reflect the empirical tendency of these configurations of roles and objectives to appear together in practice, the theoretical possibilities notwithstanding. One possible explanation for this tendency is that a practitioner faced with a delimited and concrete objective is usually working also within a more bounded time frame than one whose objective involves enhancing the functional capacity of participants. A nondirective stance is easier to sustain when there are not deadlines to meet.

A problem arises, however, when the planning practitioner is engaged in a program where *both* task and process objectives are emphasized and simultaneously pursued, as in the case of the Model Cities Program. Here the Model Cities Program guidelines set forth concrete time-bound expectations concerning completion of product components of the plan and program implementation as well as more general objectives of providing opportunities for meaningful citizen involvement in policy making, enhancing work relationships among local service-delivery units, and building problem-solving capacity.[17]

The second role dimension of task and process involves not the degree of directiveness of behavior, but the set of *primary skills* that is brought into play. The sets of skills that best characterize process and task orientations towards practice have been described as "interactional" (or sociopolitical) and "analytic" (or technical) skills, respectively.[18] *Analytic skills* involve the use of conceptual frameworks to employ systematic techniques such as investigating needs, problem definition, program design, and evaluation. *Interactional skills* involve the conscious use of self in developing social relationships, establishing lines of communication, eliciting individual and group expressions of preference, and engaging participants in decision-making procedures.

In this study we examine two of the dimensions of task and process orientations in regard to the activities of CDA directors: the degree of directiveness and control exercised; and emphasis on practice goals as reflected by the extent to which the directors' activities were focused either on achieving concrete objectives, such as design of product components within a delimited time frame, or on providing staff resources to, and mediating among, participating groups. It should be emphasized that the Model Cities Program was charged with both task (completion of a planning document and program development) and process (capacity building) objectives and that CDA directors were oriented, in varying degrees, to both sets of objectives. Our measures and discussion in this study deal with the degree of emphasis placed on these orientations, as the CDA directors described themselves, and should be interpreted in this relative sense. Thus, when we speak of "task-oriented directors," it is not to say that these people were oblivious to process, but that they tended to place less emphasis on it.

Studies of Professional Role Orientations. Generally speaking, there are two major approaches to the study of professional role orientations.[19] The first is concerned with role orientation as a dependent variable. The literature here deals with questions about the factors that influence the adoption of different role orientations. These kinds of studies analyze the ways that practitioner roles are shaped by independent variables: organizational characteristics such as objectives, degree of bureaucratization, and size; community context; competing expectations; types of clients served; and values and degree of professionalism.[20] The second approach treats role orientation as an independent variable.[21] Here, analyses focus upon the ways in which role orientations affect program outcomes, which is the approach taken in this study.

In this study we compare the CDA directors' primary role orientations during two distinct phases of the Model Cities Program—the planning period and the first action year when plans were implemented—with four outcome measures for each period. The mail survey conducted with questionnaires addressed to the CDA directors of the 147 Model Cities programs asked for ratings of the degree to which different role descriptions best characterized CDA director behaviors during the planning period and the first program year. Directors classified as *primarily task oriented* gave the highest ratings to statements that portrayed managerial and directive behaviors as follows: "administered and organized program with strong direction and high expectancy of positive response to leadership from most other actors in assigning tasks and developing product components; usually was able to achieve unity in definition and implementation of tasks to produce HUD components on schedule." Directors classified as *primarily process oriented* gave the highest ratings to statements that portrayed broker and secretariat behaviors as follows: "usually served as intermediary, referee, and mediator among actors in defining tasks and product components; acted as service agent whose prime function was not substantive but rather provided resources to whomever took leadership."

In analyzing the relationships between role orientations and program outcome, we have divided the outcome measures for each period into those associated with task and process objectives. Under task objectives are outcome variables that possess concrete time-bound attributes; here the emphases of activity are upon designing plans, obtaining funds, setting up programs, and spending funds. Under process objectives the outcome variables are more diffuse and involve building social relationships, increasing communications among groups, and facilitating citizen involvement in decision making.

The working hypothesis here is that CDA directors who were primarily task oriented would have programs that tended to rate high on achievement of task objectives and that high scores on process objectives would be associated with programs that had CDA directors who were primarily process oriented. This hypothesis is only partially supported by the findings. That is, the strongest relationships are between process orientations in the planning period and the process objectives of citizen participation (table 4-10) and between task orientations in the program year and both of the task objectives (table 4-11).

However, when we examine the planning period and program year separately, there is another trend that modifies the apparent congru-

Table 4-10. Associations Between Process/Task Orientations in Planning Period and Planning Period Outcomes

Outcomes	Gamma	N
Task Objectives		
1. Quality of CDP	+.257	57
2. Percent of Categorical Funds in CDP Budget	+.105	83
Process Objectives		
3. Coordination	+.214	69
4. Citizen Participation	+.643	81

Table 4–11. Associations Between Process/Task Orientations in First Program Year and Program Year Outcomes

Outcomes	Gamma	N
Task Objectives		
1. Quality of Program	–.739	46
2. Rate of Implementation	–.389	27
Process Objectives		
3. Coordination	–.111	39
4. Citizen Participation	–.068	44

ence between director role orientations and program outcomes. Findings for the planning period indicate that process orientations are associated positively not only with process objectives, but also with outcome measures of task objectives, albeit the latter relationships are less substantial than the former. Moving to the program year, the findings reveal that task orientations are likely to be associated with high ratings on *all* outcome measures (i.e., outcomes are negatively associated with a process orientation), even those of process objectives that have weak but nevertheless negative relationships to process orientations.

Thus, while there is some degree of congruence between task- and process-role orientations and achievement of different program objectives, the overall directions of the findings suggest that process-task *phasing* of role orientations may be the most appropriate response in programs where task and process objectives are emphasized simultaneously.

CDA Director's Professional Background

In attempting to clarify the influential factors in the relationship between administrative behavior and patterns of influence, we examined the CDA director's background. This additional piece of evidence is introduced on the assumption that CDA directors coming from different professional backgrounds would have different predispositions toward the degree of administrative control they would seek to exercise in the planning process. For example, CDA directors coming from an administrative post in a business organization might be more inclined to exercise leadership and less inclined to serve in the "secretariat" or "broker" role than a director with a background in training in the human services. If this assumption is correct, we would expect to find a relationship between the CDA director's background and his administrative behavior, in which case there would be some support for the interpretation that the directors' administrative behaviors were more a function of what they brought to the position in the way of experience and administrative predispositions than of what they encountered in the position in the way of environmental constraints and opportunities. The previous positions of CDA directors were categorized in the following way:

Urban Planning Specialist: Previous position was especially concerned with community planning, such as director of urban renewal program;

Human Service Specialist: Previous position not concerned with planning but with related functions, such as a supervisor in social work agency;

Non-Service Specialist: Previous position concerned neither with community planning nor human services, such as a businessman.

When these background data were correlated with the directors' administrative behaviors, no discernible pattern emerged to suggest that different professional backgrounds had any bearing on the directors' behaviors regarding administrative control in the Model Cities planning process. This finding suggests that the relationship between the CDA directors' administrative behavior and the MNAs' patterns of influence might be explained more in terms of an interactional effect than as a direct consequence of the CDA directors' administrative predispositions based on previous training and professional experience. That is, while the director's behavior is, by definition, partly a function of administrative predisposition, in the case of Model Cities these predispositions apparently were modified by environmental contingencies.

Changes in Directors' Role Behaviors from Planning Period to Implementation Period

In the transition from the planning period to program implementation there is reason to anticipate that some change will occur in the administrative behaviors of the CDA directors, since each period presents a different set of tasks. The direction of this change in the CDA director's administrative behavior is suggested in Blau's analysis of the difference between the dominant organizing principles for democratic and bureaucratic structures:

Bureaucratic and democratic structures can be distinguished . . . on the basis of the dominant organizing principle: efficiency or freedom of dissent. Each of these principles is suited for one purpose and not for another. When people set themselves the task of determining the social objectives that represent the interests of most of them, the crucial problem is to provide an opportunity for all conflicting viewpoints to be heard. In contrast, when the task is the achievement of given social objectives, the essential problem to be solved is to discover the most efficient, not popular, means for doing so.

Although both authoritarian elements and concessions to democratic values are found in bureaucratic structures, efficiency is the ultimate basis for evaluating whether such elements are appropriate. Disciplined obedience in the hierarchy of authority, ideally, is not valued for its own sake, . . . but is encouraged to the extent to which it contributes to effective coordination and uniform operations.[22]

Applying these principles to our problem, as the central task within the action system shifts from determining the social objectives of the community to achieving these objectives, we would anticipate a movement toward increased bureaucratization and consequent tightening of hierarchical authority, with the CDA director exercising greater administrative control over the process. Comparing the CDA directors' self-ratings of administrative behavior during the planning period and the first program year, we find that this is indeed the case. Those who rated themselves "task oriented" in the planning period switched the least: 69 percent of them also rated themselves "directive" in the program period. However, only 37 percent of those who rated themselves "process oriented" in the planning period held fast. Overall, the changes in administrative behavior that took place tended to be in the direction of task-oriented role behavior. Of the thirty-two respondents who switched their roles from the planning period to the program period, 66 percent chose task-oriented role behavior. The trend toward greater bureaucratization as the CDA moved into the first action year is also reflected in the growing size of CDA staff reported for this period.[23]

Professionalization of CDA Staff

As indicated in table 4-12, there is a moderate-positive association (gamma .297) between patterns of influence and the degree of professionalization of CDA staff, the latter defined in terms of the proportion of personnel in administrative, planning, and community organizing positions who had at least a college degree. The finding that resident influence was more likely to be strong when CDAs were staffed with a high rather than a low proportion of professionals is not surprising. During the period of the mid-1960s, the norm of professional neutrality was on the wane as the concept of the advocate planner gained prominence in professional circles.[24] In theory, the advocate planner might represent the interests of whatever group he chose to work for, be it city hall, the Defense Department, or a

Table 4-12. Degrees of Professionalization of CDA Staff (In Planning Period) and Patterns of Influence

	Degree of Professionalization of CDA Staff (percent)		
Patterns of Influence	Low (13–48)	Medium (50–65)	High (67 and over)
Staff Dominant	69.4	51.4	56.5
Parity	27.8	40.0	8.7
Resident Dominant	2.8	8.6	34.8
Total	100	100	100
	(n=36)	(n=35)	(n=23)
(gamma .297)			

neighborhood citizens' council. But in fact, it was the citizens' council in low-income neighborhoods that drew the most attention from the practitioners of advocacy planning. Aside from the norms and values of the professional culture, which at the time supported citizen influence in community planning processes, there is some evidence that among social welfare agencies, high professional density in an organization is in itself a factor related to the acceptance of professional roles that are actively committed to furthering client power and interests.[25]

The findings on CDA staff characteristics suggest that additional conflicting tendencies may be built into community agencies that have a high degree of professionalism, beyond the typical strains between administrative and professional authority anticipated in professional agencies. Professional organizations must cope regularly with a certain amount of strain because, on the one hand, administration implies a hierarchy of authority. As Etzioni puts it:

Without a clear ordering of higher and lower in rank, in which the higher in rank have more power than the lower ones and hence can control and coordinate the latter's activities, the basic principle of administration is violated; the organization ceases to be a coordinated tool.[26]

On the other hand, professional staff are employed because of the unique knowledge they possess. And a high order of individual discretion is required in the application of this knowledge to achieve organizational objectives. Professional knowledge is a source of authority quite different from the bureaucratic authority that the administrator possesses. It is the simultaneous assertion of professional and administrative authority that generally introduces a measure of strain in professional organizations. In the specific case of community planning organizations we would expect this strain to be intensified because of the relationship between professionalization and the increased sharing of decision making with citizen groups. That is, as the CDA becomes more professionalized, not only do the typical strains between bureaucratic and professional authority emerge, but a third party, the citizens' organization, is encouraged to exercise influence, based on its consumer authority. This heightened competition among consumer, professional, and bureaucratic authority was one of the distinctive features in the management of community planning efforts in Model Cities.[27]

NOTES

1. Kenneth B. Clark and Jeanette Hopkins, *A Relevant War Against Poverty: A Study of Community Action Programs and Observable Social Change* (New York: Harper and Row, 1968); and Daniel P. Moynihan, *Maximum Feasible Misunderstanding* (New York: Free Press, 1969).

2. See George Brager and Harry Specht, *Community Organizing* (New York: Columbia University Press, 1973), pp. 34-43; and Neil Gilbert and Harry Specht, *Dimensions of Social Welfare Policy* (Englewood Cliffs, N.J.: Prentice-Hall, 1974), pp. 116-17, 187-90.

3. For details of structure, see James L. Sundquist and David W. Davis, *Making Federalism Work* (Washington, D.C.: The Brookings Institution, 1969), p. 96; on process, size, and different types of subsystems, see Department of Housing and Urban Development (HUD), *The Model Cities Program: A Comparative Analysis of the Planning Process in Eleven Cities* (Washington, D.C.: Government Printing Office, 1970), on distribution of decision-making authority, see Roland L. Warren, "The Model Cities Program," *Social Welfare Forum*, 1971 (New York: Columbia University Press, 1971), pp. 140-58; on composition of CDA policy-making bodies, see Melvin Mogulof, "Black Community Development in Five Western Cities," *Social Work* 15, no. 1 (January 1970): 12-18.

4. HUD, *Administrative Performance and Capability*, CDA Letter #10A, December 1969 (Letter 10A was based on a statement by HUD Secretary Romney before the Subcommittee on Housing of the House Committee on Banking and Currency); and HUD, *Joint HUD-OEO Citizen Participation Policy for Model Cities Programs*, CDA Letter #10B, March 1970.

5. Robert K. Yin et al., *Citizen Organization: Increasing Client Control Over Services* (Santa Monica, Calif.: Rand Corp., 1973), pp. 50-51.

6. Jane Jacobs, *The Death and Life of Great American Cities* (New York: Vintage Books, 1971), pp. 130-31.

7. Tom Wolfe, *Radical Chic and Mau-Mauing the Flak Catchers* (New York: Bantam Books, 1970).

8. Harry Specht, "Disruptive Tactics," *Social Work* 14, no. 2 (April 1969): 5-15.

9. See, for example, Robert R. Alford and Eugene C. Lee, "Voting Turnover

in American Cities," *American Political Science Review* 62 (September 1968): 796-813; Richard E. Dawson and James A. Robinson, "The Politics of Welfare," in Herbert Jacob and Kenneth Vines, eds., *Politics in the American States* (Boston, Little, Brown and Co., 1965), pp. 398-401; Michael Parenti, "Ethnic Politics and the Persistence of Ethnic Identification," *American Political Science Review* 61 (September 1967); 672-683 Raymond E. Wolfinger, "The Development and Persistence of Ethnic Voting," *American Political Science Reivew* 59 (December 1965): 896-908.

10. Robert L. Lineberry and Edmund P. Fowler, "Reformism and Public Policies in American Cities," *American Political Science Review* 61 (September 1967): 701-716.

11. Brager and Specht, pp. 184-85; Sherry Arnstein, "A Ladder of Citizen Participation," *Journal of the American Institute of Planners* 35, no. 4 (July 1969): 221-22; Roland Warren, "Model Cities First Round: Politics, Planning, and Participation," *Journal of the American Institute of Planners* 35, no. 4 (July 1969): 247.

12. H. Ralph Taylor, "Remarks Before the Meeting of the National Association of Housing and Redevelopment Officials," Minneapolis, Minnesota, 27 September, 1968; quoted in Sunquist and Davis, p. 94.

13. For a more detailed discussion of this issue see, Neil Gilbert and Harry Specht, "Social Planning and Community Organization," *Encyclopedia of Social Work*, ed. John Turner (New York: National Association of Social Workers, 1977), pp. 1404-1424.

14. NASW Committee on Community Organization, *Defining Community Organization Practice* (New York: NASW, 1962).

15. Jack Rothman, "An Analysis of Goals and Roles in Community Organization Practice," *Social Work* 9, no. 2 (April 1964): 26.

16. Ibid.

17. For the specific formulation of these objectives, see U.S. Department of Housing and Urban Development, *Improving the Quality of Urban Life: A Program Guide to Model Neighborhoods in Demonstration Cities* (Washington, D.C.: Government Printing Office, 1966).

18. This dimension of task and process is discussed and analyzed in Ralph M. Kramer and Harry Specht, eds., *Readings in Community Organization Practice*, 2d ed. (Englewood Cliffs, N.J.: Prentice-Hall, Inc., 1975), p. 6; Brager and Specht; Robert Perlman and Arnold Gurin, *Community Organization and Social Planning* (New York: John Wiley and Sons, (1972); Irwin T. Sanders, "Professional Roles in Planned Change," in Kramer and Specht, pp. 291-99; and Neil Gilbert and Harry Specht, eds., *Planning for Social Welfare* (Englewood Cliffs, N.J.: Prentice-Hall, Inc.. 1977).

19. For an overview of the research literature on practitioner roles see Jack Rothman, *Planning and Organizing for Social Change* (New York: Columbia University Press, 1977), pp. 35-107.

20. For example, see Ralph M. Kramer, "Ideology Status and Power in Board Executive Relationships," in Kramer and Specht; Edwin J. Thomas, "Role Conceptions and Organizational Size," *American Sociological Review* 20, no. 1 (February 1959): 30-37; Robert K. Merton, *Social Theory and Social Structure*

(Glencoe, Ill.: The Free Press, 1957), pp. 195-224; Perlman and Gurin; Benjamin Paul, *Health Culture and Community* (New York: Russell Sage Foundation, 1955); Neil Gilbert, *Clients or Constituents* (San Francisco: Jossey Bass, 1970), pp. 69-90; Elizabeth McBroom, "Helping AFDC Families—A Comparative Study," *Social Service Review* 39, no. 4 (December 1965): 390-98; and Irwin Epstein, "Professionalization, Professionalism and Social-Worker Radicalism," *Journal of Health and Social Behavior* 11, no. 1 (March 1970): 67-77.

21. For example, Brett W. Hawkins, et al., "A Macro-Analysis of the Effects of Planning Agency Professionalism on Municipal Planning Outputs," *Journal of the American Institute of Planners* 41, no. 2 (June 1975): 419-26; and Irving Spergel, *Community Problem Solving: The Delinquency Example* (Chicago: University of Chicago Press, 1969).

22. Peter M. Blau, *Bureaucracy in Modern Society* (New York: Random House, 1956), pp. 105-106.

23. Empirical studies of the relationship between organizational size and bureaucratization indicate that size tends to be associated with the enhancement of some bureaucratic characteristics such as complexity, differentiation, and formal structuring of activity. On other characteristics, such as centralization of authority, the evidence is inconclusive. For example, see Richard Hall, J. Eugene Haas, and Norman J. Johnson, "Organizational Size, Complexity, and Formalization," *American Sociological Review* 32, no. 6 (December 1967): 901-912; D.S. Pugh, D. Hickson, C.R. Hinings, and C. Turner, "The Context of Organizational Structure," *Administrative Science Quarterly* 14, no. 1 (March 1969): 91-114; and P. Montagna, "Professionalization and Bureaucratization in Large Professional Organizations," *American Journal of Sociology* 74, no. 2 (1968): 138-45.

24. For example, see Paul Davidoff, "Advocacy and Pluralism in Planning," *Journal of the American Institute of Planners* 31, no. 4 (November 1965): 331-38.

25. Jack Rothman, et al., *Guidelines for Social Change: Utilization of Social Science Research in Social Planning and Community Action*, A Report of a Research Project Sponsored by National Institute of Mental Health, University of Michigan, 1972, part 2, p. 55 (Interim Draft).

26. Amitai Etzioni, *Modern Organizations* (Englewood Cliffs, N.J.: Prentice Hall, Inc., 1964), p. 76.

27. For an analysis of the values underlying this process see Neil Gilbert, Armin Rosenkranz, and Harry Specht, "The Dialectics of Social Planning," *Social Work* 18, no. 2 (March 1973): 78-86.

※ **Chapter 5**

Patterns of Influence and the Chain of Planning Objectives

In the previous chapter we examined the ways in which different characteristics of the action system were associated with the achievement of varying degrees of citizen influence. We turn now to an analysis of the relationships between degrees of citizen influence in the planning process and other links in the Model Cities "chain of planning objectives." The chain of planning objectives consists of: *a planning process* involving a high degree of citizen influence which leads to the development of: (1) a high quality *Comprehensive Demonstration Plan* (CDP) containing clearly stated and innovative policies derived from rational analysis to guide; (2) *a process of implementation* involving a high degree of coordination of services and citizen participation that leads to; (3) a high quality of *performance* in establishing programs aimed at improving the quality of life in urban communities.

This chain of planning objectives represents a theoretical model that assumes that each link is connected to the next in line. It is possible, of course, that none of these objectives is related, or that some are inversely related, or that the chain is composed really of only two or three of these objectives. The relationships *among* the objectives will be examined in chapter 8. In this section we are interested only in the connections between patterns of influence and these other objectives: the quality of the CDP, the desired process of implementation, and program performance in the first action year.

PATTERNS OF INFLUENCE AND THE
QUALITY OF THE CDP

The CDPs contained three major components: a problem analysis; a statement of priorities (derived from the problem analysis); and specific project proposals for a comprehensive attack on the combined physical and social ills of Model Neighborhoods. The project proposals were the actual plans for the programs to be developed during the first action year. These proposals involved efforts to develop programs in the functional areas of housing, relocation, social services, health, education, transportation, manpower, training, and the like. An estimate of the overall breakdown of HUD's *proposed* funding of these fuctional areas in Model Cities is shown in figure 5-1.

Project descriptions in the CDPs were expected to include: (1) designations of the sponsoring agency; (2) plans for coordination of agencies; (3) a structure for citizen participation; (4) budget summaries; and (5) some indication of funding sources other than Model

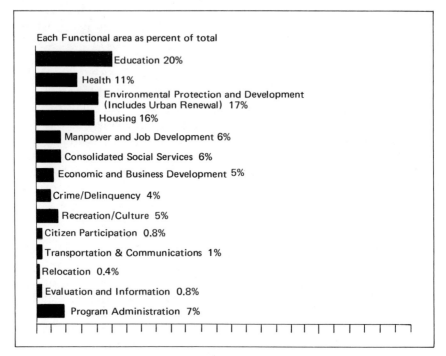

Figure 5-1. Functional Designation of Funds Based on Project Summaries

Source: *Model Cities: A Report on Progress: Special Issue of the Model Cities Service Center Bulletin.* 2, no. 9 (June 1971): 41.

Cities supplemental monies that would be committed to the program.

In this analysis, five broad criteria are used to assess the quality of the CDPs:

1. HUD officials' judgments of the "best/worst" CDPs;
2. the proportion of categorical funds included in the CDP budget;
3. the proportion of local funds included in the CDP budget;
4. judgments of the *quality* of agency participation in planning for the CDP; and
5. the number of agencies designated in the CDP as having formal responsibility for carrying out proposed projects.

These criteria reflect general features of the CDPs, but not the *substantive* qualities of the CDPs, which would be much more difficult to compare systematically.

Judgments of "Best/Worst" CDPs

The HUD deskmen were asked to select from among the cities under their jurisdiction those that produced what they considered to be the "best" CDPs (plans that impressed the deskmen most positively) and those that produced the "worst" CDPs (plans that impressed the deskmen most negatively). Although positive ratings outweighed negative rating by almost two-to-one, this should not be interpreted to mean that a larger proportion of cities produced CDPs that met HUD's rigorous standards and high expectations. On the contrary, few CDPs approached the *ideal* product envisioned by HUD officials. What these ratings indicate is the *relative* quality of an individual CDP in comparison to the general level of competence reflected in the other CDPs.

When asked to describe the features of the CDP upon which they based their positive and negative judgments, the HUD administrators responses varied. According to their comments, the CDPs rated "best" were clearly written documents; made some effort to connect the parts (problem analysis, priorities, strategy, and project proposals) at least in the abstract; were not oriented to physical planning alone; indicated at least theoretical relationships among the projects; contained, perhaps, a few interesting or innovative ideas; and most important of all, seemed reasonably workable. Examples of what were considered innovative projects included: a city's plan for a transit loop system to tie in with the existing bus system in order to provide MNA residents with a quick and convenient mode of urban transportation; a plan for a library that would lend work tools to MNA residents who wanted to make home repairs; and a plan for incentive bonuses for MNA teachers. The most frequent descriptions of the "best"CDPs referred to them as "do-able," "workable," and "realistic."

The reverse was true for those CDPs rated "worst." For example, some of the following comments describe the "worst" CDPs:

It contained ninety-three projects, a real pie-in-the-sky operation.

It defined five subneighborhoods with separate plans for each and ended up asking for five of everything.

Its projects were identical to those produced by another city in that State—looked like the pages were Xeroxed right out of the other city's CDP.

Weak project descriptions; poor budget; it was not an operational document.

When the cities' CDP ratings (made by HUD deskmen) are correlated with patterns of influence, notable differences emerge (table 5-1). These data reveal that cities with parity patterns of influence were most likely to produce CDPs judged to be relatively high quality compared to all other cities. While the "best/worst" ratio for all cities is 1.68, a little less than two-to-one, the "best/worst" ratio in parity cities is over four-to-one. The resident-dominant cities were least likely to produce high-quality CDPs; reversing the overall "best/worst" ratio, the ratio for resident-dominant cities is close to one-to-two. That is, resident-dominant cities were likely to produce CDPs judged in the "worst" category almost twice as often as CDPs in the "best" category.

Proportion of Categorical Funds in the CDPs

The extent to which CDAs were able to attain commitments from agencies to support the specific programs proposed in the CDP is reflected in the proportion of the CDP budget composed of categorical funds. (The proportion of supplemental funds is that part of the CDP budget given as a bloc grant to the CDA by the Model Cities Agency.) While the proportion of categorical funds does not tell us whether the CDAs actually received and spent these funds, it does give us some relative measure of the CDAs' ability to create a plan that involved the concentration and mobilization of resources from related programs, one of HUD's major objectives for Model Cities planning.

Table 5-1. Patterns of Influence and Ratios of "Best/Worst" CDPs

Patterns of Influence	Best CDPs (percent)	Worst CDPs (percent)	Best/Worst Ratio
Staff Dominant	62 (n=36)	38 (n=22)	1.64
Parity	82 (n=22)	19 (n=5)	4.32
Resident Dominant	35 (n=6)	65 (n=11)	.55
All Cities	63 (n=64)	37 (n=38)	1.68

There is a weak positive association (gamma .126) between patterns of influence and the percent of categorical funds in the CDP budget. While this finding indicates that there is no substantial linear relationship between the two variables, the distribution in table 5-2 reveals that cities with parity patterns of influence were far more likely to have CDPs in the high range of categorical funding than either staff-dominant or resident-dominant cities: 57 percent of the parity cities reported a high percent (33 percent or more) of categorical funds in their CDP budgets compared to one-third of the resident-dominant cities and one-fourth of the staff-dominant cities.

Proportion of Local Funds in the CDP Budget

As we noted in chapter 3, the percent of local funds in the CDP budget gives some indication of generalized local political support for the Model Cities Program. We find that there is a low-negative association (gamma -.161) between the percent of local contributions and citizen influence (table 5-3).[a] But the interesting feature of the relationship is that staff-dominant cities were more likely than others to attain higher percentages of local funds, whereas the parity cities were the most likely to come out with higher percentages of categorical funds. This occurred, we believe, because the staff-dominant CDAs were more likely to be run as instruments of the cities' executives and, therefore, were given more local support. The parity CDAs are somewhat more independent of the city in order to carry out their integrating function among agencies, citizens, and government. For that reason they are more likely to be working actively and

[a]Local contributions constituted a less significant proportion of CDP budgets than categorical funds. Local funds were *less than* 10 percent of the budgets in two-thirds of the cities; categorical funds were *more than* 12 percent of the budgets in three-fourths of the cities.

Table 5-2. Patterns of Influence and Percent of Categorical Funds in the CDP

| Percent Categorical Funds in CDP | Patterns of Influence | | |
	Staff Dominant (percent)	Parity (percent)	Resident Dominant (percent)
Low (0–12)	33	22	60
Medium (13–32)	43	22	7
High (33 or more)	24	57	33
Total	100	101[a]	100
	(n=66)	(n=28)	(n=15)
(gamma .126)			

[a]due to rounding

cooperatively with the agencies from which categorical funds are obtained.

Quality of Agency Participation in Planning

The quality of agency participation in planning (as judged by the deskmen in Washington and the leadmen in the regions) does not bear a linear correlation to degree of citizen influence in planning. This can be noted in table 5-4 where the association between these variables is -.065. However, if we examine the relationships within table 5-4, it is clear that parity systems of citizen influence were more likely to be given high ratings in quality of agency participation by deskmen and leadmen than other systems of influence. Fifty percent of parity cities were rated high in regard to quality of agency participation in planning compared to 22.7 percent of high ratings for resident-dominant cities and 29 percent for staff-dominant cities.

Table 5-3. Patterns of Influence and Percent of Local Funds in the CDP Budget

| Percent Local Funds In CDP | Patterns of Influence | | |
	Staff Dominant (percent)	Parity (percent)	Resident Dominant (percent)
Low (0–2)	28.8	35.7	46.7
Medium (3–9)	37.9	36.7	26.7
High (10–60)	33.3	28.6	26.7
Total	100	101[a]	100.1[a]
	(n=66)	(n=28)	(n=15)
(gamma −.161)			

[a]due to rounding

Table 5-4. Patterns of Influence and Quality of Agency Participation in Planning

Agency Participation In Planning	Patterns of Influence		
	Staff Dominant (percent)	Parity (percent)	Resident-Dominant (percent)
Low	18.8	18.75	50
Medium	52.2	31.25	27.3
High	29	50	22.7
Total	100	100	100
	(n=69)	(n=32)	(n=42)
(gamma –.065)			

Number of Agencies in the CDP

The number of agencies in the CDP designated to assume formal responsibility for carrying out proposed Model Cities projects reflects a quantitative dimension of the "degree of coordination effort" that the plan required; that is, the larger the number of agencies in the plan, the greater the effort necessary to coordinate activities during the program implementation phase. In using this variable as an indicator of CDP quality we are assuming that cities with CDPs that designated a higher number of agencies committed to projects (at least on paper) were responding to HUD's coordination objective more forcefully than cities with CDPs that required program implementation involving a lesser number of agencies.

Examining the association between number of agencies in the CDP and patterns of influence in planning, we find a weak-negative relationship (gamma –.116). Among the CDPs with the highest number of agencies committed to projects, staff-dominant and parity patterns of influence were represented almost equally, while resident-dominant patterns of influence were substantially underrepresented (table 5-5). These findings lend limited support to the proposition (cited in chapter 2) that the number of agencies participating in the Model Cities planning process will vary inversely with degree of citizen influence in planning.

However, because CDAs in large cities have a much greater number of agencies to draw upon that those in small cities, it is possible that city size might have influenced these findings. We explore the impact that city size has on agency participation in chapter 7.

PATTERNS OF INFLUENCE AND THE IMPLEMENTATION PROCESS

The relationships between patterns of influence during the planning

Table 5-5. Patterns of Influence and Number of Agencies in the CDP

| | Patterns of Influences | | |
Number of Agencies	Staff Dominant (percent)	Parity (percent)	Resident Dominant (percent)
Low (0-6)	35	39	33
Medium (7-11)	32	32	53
High (12-31)	33	29	13
Total	100	100	99[a]
	(n=66)	(n=28)	(n=15)
(gamma –.116)			

[a] due to rounding

period and two major features of the implementation process (citizen participation and agency coordination) are shown in tables 5-6 and 5-7. As we would anticipate, there is a strong positive relationship (gamma .682) between patterns of influence during planning, and citizen participation in the first action year. This finding is expected, if for no other reason than that citizen groups with some degree of decision-making power in the planning phase would certainly seek to build mechanisms into the CDP for their continued involvement in implementation. In any case, it would seem difficult to eliminate citizen involvement just at the point that the payoff of their planning activities materializes. (Difficult, but not impossible, as indicated by the 22 percent of resident-dominant cities that received "poor" ratings on citizen participation in the action year.)

At the other extreme, in cities where citizen influence in the planning phase was negligible there is little reason to assume that citizen groups would suddenly arise and press for a strong hand in implementation. Indeed, as the data reveal, only 2 percent of the staff-dominant cities were rated high in the achievement of citizen participation in the first action year. It is especially interesting to note that none of the parity cities received poor ratings on citizen

Table 5-6. Patterns of Influence and Implementation of Citizen Participation

| | Patterns of Influence | | |
Implementation of Citizen Participation	Staff Dominant (percent)	Parity (percent)	Resident Dominant (percent)
Poor	41	—	22
Fair	57	47	56
Excellent	2	53	22
Total	100	100	100
	(n=46)	(n=19)	(n=9)
(gamma .682)			

participation, and 53 percent of them received excellent ratings on their achievement of citizen participation. Moreover, a larger proportion of parity cities than of resident-dominant cities were rated high on this objective.

As indicated in table 5-7, there is a moderate-positive association (gamma .357) between patterns of influence and the implementation of service coordination objectives. Staff-dominant cities did somewhat better on this objective (14 percent were rated excellent) than on citizen participation, and resident-dominant cities did somewhat worse (only 10 percent were rated excellent). Again, parity cities surpassed the others, none having poor ratings and 31 percent being in the excellent category.

PATTERNS OF INFLUENCE AND PERFORMANCE

While comprehensive rational planning, citizen participation, and coordination were ends to be pursued in their own right, in a fundamental sense they were also means to the more inclusive goal of improving the quality of life in urban communities. Planning, participation, and coordination each might contribute to this objective, but the final test is how successful the Model Cities were in creating and implementing effective programs to serve the designated communities. Two measures of program performance are used to assess the achievement of this objective and how it relates to the patterns of influence in the planning process. The first measure is the extent to which programs that were planned and funded were finally implemented, as reflected in Model Cities spending patterns for the first action year. The second measure involves the judgments of HUD officials of the relative success achieved by the different cities in their programs.

Table 5-7. **Patterns of Influence and Implementation of Service Coordination Objectives**

| Implementation of Coordination Objectives | Patterns of Influence | | |
	Staff Dominant (percent)	Parity (percent)	Resident Dominant (percent)
Poor	34	—	20
Fair	52	69	70
Excellent	14	31	10
Total	100	100	100
	(n=44)	(n-13)	(n=10)
(gamma .357)			

Spending Patterns

One indicator of a city's performance in implementing programs is its ability to spend the funds awarded to it. Whatever else it may be doing, a city that manages to spend only a small percent of its first-year grant is not doing much in the way of program implementation. While it may seem a simple matter to spend a few million dollars on new programs, administrative and organizational skills are required, and, in fact, most Model Cities had a difficult time spending the money. The virtue of spending as an indicator of performance is that it is an objective measure and not subject to distortion by the perceptions and beliefs of raters. But spending is a rather gross measure which does not tap the qualitative and subtle nuances of program performance. Conceivably, cities that score high on this performance measure may, in reality, be spending program monies in the way that Othello loved—not wisely, but too well. However, in that a modicum of administrative and organizational skills are necessary to create a programmatic framework for spending money, we assume that cities that scored high on this indicator possessed at least as much wisdom with regard to program development as those that scored low.

Our figures for spending refer to the supplementary funds that HUD awarded to cities for their first program year. The data, which were gathered in September 1971, include the six-month spending of 112 cities, the twelve-month spending of sixty-three cities, and the per capita twelve-month expenditures of sixty-one cities.[b]

Overall, spending appears to have been a problem for the cities. Only one-third of the cities that had been operating the program for twelve months were able to spend 50 percent or more of their funds; conversely, after twelve months, two-thirds of the cities had spent less than half the funds that had been allocated to them for the first program year. There is some evidence that spending performance improves with time since the picture of twelve-month spending, while bleak, is a considerable improvement over the picture at six months. That is, at six months, 80 percent of the cities had spent only between 3 and 23 percent of their funds (table 5-8).

The relationships between patterns of influence in the planning year and the spending rates for cities at six months, twelve months, and per capita at twelve months of the first program year are given in

[b] Cities began their first program year at different times and therefore were at different spending periods when the study was done. Per capita expenditures were derived by dividing the twelve-months of program expenditures by the MNA population. The per capita twelve-month expenditures, we believe, give the most refined measure of spending performance in that they take account of the size of the population for which expenditures were made.

Table 5-8. Percentages of Supplemental Funds Spent by Model Cities at Six Months and Twelve Months

Percent of Supplemental Funds Spent	Percent of Cities Achieving This Expenditure Level At Six Months	Percent of Cities Achieving This Expenditure Level At Twelve Months
10 or less	22	
23 or less	80	
35 or less		32
50 or less	100	67
95 or less		100
	(n=112)	(n=63)

table 5-9. Here the cities are rated by the proportions achieving *low* scores on each of the spending measures. These data reveal that more of the parity cities than others were able to spend higher proportions of their grants, while approximately the same proportions of resident-dominant and staff-dominant cities were likely to have poor spending performance.

Qualitative Judgments of Performance

Deskmen were asked to identify those cities that, in their judgments, operated the "most successful" first-year programs and those cities that operated the "least successful" first-year programs. In all, they rated eighty-three cities, forty-eight "most successful" and thirty-five "least successful." The criteria given by raters for placing cities in the "most" or "least" successful categories included the degree of achievement of HUD process objectives such as coordination and citizen participation. Particular emphasis was put upon the speed and quality of program implementation. The deskmen expressed the least enthusiasm about the program performance of cities in which implementation was sluggish. The distributions of "most/ least" ratings to cities with different patterns of influence are listed in table 5-10.

The data in table 5-10 show that parity cities emerge with the highest success ratio in terms of overall performance ratings for the first program year followed, in order, by staff-dominant cities and resident-dominant cities. Parity cities are judged to be "most successful" in their program performance almost four times as often as they were judged "least successful" compared to staff-dominant cities which were judged "most successful" only 1.5 times as often as "least successful;" resident-dominant cities, on the other hand, were judged "least successful" more than twice as often as they were judged "most successful." These results are consistent with the other findings on the relationship between patterns of citizen influence in planning and the achievement of first-year program objectives.

Table 5-9. Patterns of Influence and the Percentages of Cities With Low Rates of Spending at Six Months, Twelve Months, and Per Capita Spending at Twelve Months

	Patterns of Influence		
	Staff Dominance (percent)	Parity (percent)	Resident Dominant (percent)
Proportion Spending 23 percent or less at Six Months	79 (n=67)	75 (n=28)	94 (n-17)
Proportion Spending 51 percent or less at Twelve Months	68 (n=40)	57 (n=14)	77 (n-9)
Proportion Spending $49 Per Capita or less at Twelve Months	42 (n=33)	22 (n=9)	40 (n=5)

Table 5-10. Patterns of Influence and "Most/Least Successful" First-Year Programs

Patterns of Influence	Most Successful (percent)	Least Successful (percent)	Total	Most/Least Ratio
Staff Dominant	60 (n=28)	40 (n=19)	100	1.47
Parity	71 (n=15)	29 (n=4)	100	3.75
Resident Dominant	29 (n=5)	71 (n=12)	100	.42
All Cities	58 (n=48)	42 (n=35)	100	1.37

SUMMARY

The creation of a community planning network that involved a strong element of citizen participation was an initial link in the chain of Model Cities planning objectives. While HUD staff held different interpretations as to whether a "strong element" implied that citizen groups were to have controlling influence or an equal share in decision making, a staff-dominant planning arrangement clearly did not satisfy this objective. Still, different planning arrangements ranging from staff-dominant patterns of influence to resident-dominant patterns of influence developed in different communities. In chapter 4 we examined a series of demographic, organizational, staff, and sociopolitical elements in the action system and their relationships to the patterns of influence that emerged in the planning period. In analyzing the action system we asked the following question: What characteristics are associated with the development of different kinds of citizen-influence patterns in the planning process? The purpose here was to try to understand the conditions under which the first link in the chain-of-planning-objectives was forged.

In brief, we found the following:

Demographic characteristics: Patterns of influence had no relationship to the racial composition of the Model Neighborhood Area (MNA) but did vary directly with its size; that is, MNAs with larger populations were more likely to develop strong citizen influence than MNAs with small populations.

Organizational arrangements: There was a moderate-positive association between patterns of influence and the extent to which resident-organization staff were independent of the CDA; that is, the more control that resident organizations had over their staff the greater the probability that citizen influence would be strong.

CDA staff characteristics: The CDA directors' exercise of administrative control was unrelated to their professional backgrounds, but varied with patterns of influence in the anticipated direction. That is, in action systems where citizen influence was strong the CDA directors rated themselves as exercising less administrative control than in systems where staff-dominant patterns prevailed. Also, resident influence was more likely to occur in action systems in which the proportion of professionals on CDA staffs were high than in systems where there were comparatively fewer professionals on the CDA staff. Moreover, we found that CDA directors who were process oriented were more likely to be successful at all planning-periods tasks and CDA directors who were technically oriented were more likely than others to be successful at all implementation-period tasks. However, interpretation of this finding must be balanced by the fact that technically-oriented directors were most successful at technical tasks and the process-oriented directors were most successful at process tasks.

Sociopolitical environment: The development of each of the patterns of influence was associated with a different combination of conflict and political integration in the environment. Staff-dominant patterns of influence occurred most frequently in sociopolitical environments that were dormant, characterized by low conflict and low political integration; parity patterns of influence developed in stable environments, characterized by low-to-moderate degrees of conflict and high degrees of political integration; and resident-dominant patterns were usually found in turbulent sociopolitical environments where conflict was high and political integration low. It should be noted that in this analysis we looked at the sociopolitical environments at a fixed point in time. A longitudinal study of the experiences in these environments might well reveal that *over time* there is a dynamic relationship between conflict and political integration. It is not unlikely that, in the process of community change, an intensification of conflict *precedes* an increase in political integration; that is, in sociopolitical environments in which there is low political integration, social conflict may be a necessary prerequisite for the creation of new sociopolitical arrangements.

In this chapter we have considered how different patterns of influence in the planning process relate to the achievement of other Model Cities planning objectives. Various measures were used to assess planning outcomes, including the quality of the Comprehensive Demonstration Plan that was produced, the process of program implementation, and the quality of program performance. The findings here indicate that cities characterized by parity patterns of influence do better on all the outcome measures than other cities. Cities with resident-dominant patterns of influence do poorest on almost all measures of outcome. And cities with staff-dominant patterns of influence fall in between the other two on almost all outcome measures.

These findings are of particular interest because of the uncertainty about the relative emphasis on parity versus resident-dominant patterns of influence as the initial objective in the design of Model Cities planning networks. In the name of participatory democracy a case can be made for the achievement of the resident-dominant pattern as valuable in its own right. However, as a program objective that is *both* means and end it must not only be valued on its own, but also proven to be instrumental to the achievement of other valued objectives. Clearly this was not shown to be the case in Model Cities. Similarly, the evidence for the utility of staff-dominant patterns on the basis of their instrumental value seems lacking. The parity pattern of influence is, by comparison, a planning arrangement for which the claim may be made legitimately that citizens do participate because they share with, exchange with, and build relationships with political leaders, agencies, and professionals. Though they do not achieve the same degree of self-determination as resident-dominant patterns, the parity arrangements are far superior to the others as an instrumental value.

"Citizen participation" has many meanings. Our findings suggest that when citizen participation is defined in terms of the parity arrangement it is an important element in achieving success in community planning.

✳ Chapter 6

The Interorganizational Field

The City Demonstration Agency's (CDA's) interorganizational field consists of the other public and private human-service organizations in the Model City, and the city's chief executive (the mayor or city manager, depending on which had formal legal authority over the CDA director). While the other human-service organizations are clearly part of the interorganizational field, the chief exeuctive could be viewed as part of the action system, interorganizational field, or community context. We choose to include the chief executive in the analysis of the interorganizational field because he is in the best position to mediate relationships among community agencies as well as between community agencies and agencies external to the community. Thus, the chief executive has significant potential to impact on other elements in the interorganizational field.

In chapters 4 and 5 we discussed the action system both as a dependent variable (being "caused by" sociopolitical and demographic factors such as degree of conflict and proportions of racial minorities) and as an independent variable (as a "cause of" the other elements in the Department of Housing and Urban Development's chain of planning objectives). In this chapter we will consider the interorganizational field variables as independent and dependent. Although we must begin with the assumption that the interorganizational field existed prior to the Model Cities Program, one can view these relationships as dynamic in the sense that the interorganizational fields affected the ways in which the Model Cities Programs developed, and Model Cities also had an effect upon the interorgani-

zational field. The case for a dynamic perspective on these relationships is strong in regard to analysis of the associations between the
interorganizational field and the action system, particularly between
patterns of citizen influence and quality of agency participation in
planning, and number of agencies participating. Thus, in our analysis
we will examine behaviors of the action system and developments in
the interorganizational field as evolving together, each affecting
the other.

DIMENSIONS OF THE
INTERORGANIZATIONAL FIELD

We will use three measures to describe the basic dimensions of the
interorganizational field. These are: chief executive commitment,
quality of agency participation in planning, and number of agencies
involved in planning. The associations among these interorganizational characteristics, given in table 6-1, suggest that the three measures
are not in any degree equivalent indicators of the same phenomena.
That is, there is a moderate-positive degree of association between
chief executive commitment and *quality* of agency participation in
planning (gamma .432). But there is a low-negative association between chief executive commitment and *number* of agencies in planning (gamma -.172); and there is a negligible-negative association
between *quality* of agency participation in planning and *number* of
agencies in planning (gamma -.059). The differences in the association among these pairs of variables constitute an interesting aspect of
the analysis of the interorganizational field. When we analyze the relationships among these variables and the HUD planning objectives,
the important differences between *quality* of agency participation in
planning and *numbers* of agencies participating in planning will
become clear.

The investigation of the interorganizational field is structured by a
framework similar to the one employed in analysis of the action system in chapter 5 (figure 6-1).

Table 6-1.   Associations Between Interorganizational Field Variables (gammas)

	Quality of Agency Participation In Planning	*Number of Agencies Participating In Planning*
Chief Executive	.432	-.172
Quality of Agency Participation In Planning	—	-.059

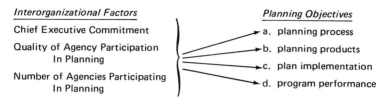

Figure 6-1. Relationships Between Interorganizational Field Variables and Planning Objectives

Before examining the relationships between interorganizational factors and planning objectives, let us take a closer look at the types of agencies involved in the interorganizational field.

Types of Agencies and Levels of Involvement

The frequency with which different types of agencies were involved in some aspect of Model Cities planning and coordination is shown in table 6-2. Based on reports from 112 Model Cities, the first column in the table indicates the numbers of cities in which each of these types of organizations was involved in one or more of the following ways: played a role in the planning process; agreed to a formal program role in the Comprehensive Demonstration Plan (CDP); and played an active role in program implementation during the first action year. As the data reveal, the most frequent participants were public agencies: boards of education, departments of health, probation/correction/police agencies, city planning, and recreation departments. The bottom half of the list is composed mainly of private organizations such as churches, family service agencies, colleges, and health and welfare councils which, on the whole, were much less likely to be involved in planning and implementation than public agencies.[a]

Why were private organizations less likely to participate? Previous discussion of the interorganizational field (pp. 36-39) suggests three reasons that may partially explain this phenomenon. First, some private organizations, such as industries, colleges, and chambers of commerce, are not typically considered to be within the task environment of social service agencies. Introducing these types of organizations into planning and service-coordination networks probably requires greater effort and more adjustments in the existing domain consensus than is the case with traditional social welfare organiza-

---

[a]"Social Planning Department" is the agency type that was reported to participate least frequently by the 112 cities. However, we believe that this is because most cities do not have this kind of department, and that it is not a reflection of the degree of which this type of agency participates.

Table 6-2.   Types of Agencies, Numbers of Cities in Which Each Type Participated, and Intensity of Participation

Types of Agencies	Number of Cities in Which Type of Agency Participated	Intense Participation (Percent that participated in all aspects of planning and implementation)	Limited Participation (Percent that participated only in planning)
Board of Education	107	69.2	4.7
Department of Health	102	52	19.6
Corrections/Probation/Police	96	47.9	16.7
City Planning	94	42.5	31.9
Recreation	90	50	8.9
Urban Renewal	84	52.4	14.3
Department of Welfare	83	36.1	36.1
Public Employment Service	83	33.7	25.3
Public Housing	81	32.1	29.6
Office of Economic Opportunity	81	53.1	18.5
Civic and Voluntary Agency	72	40.3	29.2
Church	71	31	38
Family Service Agency	64	35.9	26.6
Chamber of Commerce	45	20	37.8
Department of Transportation	40	30	42.5
Personnel Department	40	35	22.5
Health and Welfare Council	39	15.4	48.7
Private Industry	34	26.5	50
College	29	72.4	10.3
Social Planning Department	18	33	22.2

tions. Second, political leaders have less leverage with private organizations than with public organizations in which they are important members of the input constituency. Thus, in communities where political leadership strongly supported the Model Cities Program, pressures to participate could be exerted upon public agencies more effectively than upon private agencies. Finally, in getting involved with the CDA, public agencies may have felt their autonomy to be less threatened than private agencies. For private agencies, participation in Model Cities meant that their input constituency would be expanded in varying degrees to include the CDA, local political leadership, and citizen participants. Although the private agencies might obtain new funds, in the process they would also become increasingly accountable to these new input constituencies. Generally, public agencies are more accustomed to being accountable to these constituencies.

The levels of participation of different types of agencies, which are listed in the second and third columns of table 6-2, suggest that the costs of participation were felt more intensely by private organizations than by public organizations. The second column gives the percentages of each type that participated in all three aspects of the process (i.e., "intense participation:" played a role in planning; agreed to a formal program role in the CDA; and played an active role in implementation). The ten types of agencies in the upper part of the table (those with the highest frequencies of participation in the 112 cities, *all* of which are public agencies) have a greater intensity of participation overall than the ten types in the lower part of the table (those with the lowest frequencies of participation, *most* of which are private organizations). The average percentage of intense participation for the first ten types is 48 percent compared to a 33 percent average of intense participation for the second ten types.

The third column is almost the converse of the second column. These figures show the percentages of each type that participated *only* in the planning aspect of the Model Cities Program ("limited participation"). The average percentage of limited participation for the ten types in the upper part of the table is 20 percent compared to a 34 percent average percentage of limited participation for the second ten types. Thus, not only were private agencies on the whole less likely to participate than public agencies, but the participation of private agencies was more likely to be of a limited nature, and they tended to withdraw more often than public agencies after the initial involvement in the planning period.

The lower overall rates of participation for private organizations might be due to the difficulty of involving nontraditional organizations in social planning and to the CDA's relatively weak political leverage on private organizations as compared to public organizations. The higher withdrawal rates after the planning period of private agencies that participated in planning suggests, in addition, that when private organizations actually got involved in planning and had the opportunity to assess the costs and benefits of participation, many of them may have concluded that the former would be greater than the latter.

INTERORGANIZATIONAL FIELD VARIABLES AND THE CHAIN OF PLANNING OBJECTIVES

The Action System

At first look it appears that the relationships between interorganizational factors and the pattern of influence are either negligible or low-negative. In table 6-3 we give the associations between the three interorganizational variables and patterns of influence. The associations between patterns of influence and chief executive commitment, and between patterns of influence and quality of agency participation in planning are both negligible (gammas .064 and -.065, respectively), and the association between patterns of influence and the numbers of agencies participating in planning is low-negative (gamma -.154). However, when we explore these associations in more detail, we find that the high degrees of executive commitment to the Model Cities Program and high quality of agency participation in planning are most likely to be found in cities that developed parity planning systems.

Chief Executive Commitment: While the degree of association between chief executive commitment and patterns of influence is negligible, examination of the data in table 6-4 suggests that strong executive commitment occurred most frequently in cities that developed parity influence systems and least frequently in resident-dominant cities. A tentative explanation for this difference concerns

Table 6-3. Associations Between Interorganizational Field Variables and Patterns of Influence (Gammas)

	Interorganizational Field Variables		
	Chief Executive Commitment	*Quality of Agency Participation In Planning*	*Number of Agencies Participating In Planning*
Patterns of Influence	.064	-.065	-.154

Table 6-4. Chief Executive Commitment and Patterns of Influence

| | Chief Executive Commitment | | |
Patterns of Influence	Weak (percent)	Moderate (percent)	Strong (percent)
Staff-Dominant	50.0	58.6	36.4
Parity	18.2	26.8	40.9
Resident-Dominant	31.8	14.6	22.7
Total	100	100	100
	(n=22)	(n=41)	(n=22)
(gamma .064)			

the ways in which chief executive commitment may be affected by degree of MNA conflict and political integration in the action system. That is, in cities where there are low-to-moderate degrees of conflict and high degrees of political integration, chief executive involvement in the program is encouraged. These cities are most likely to be characterized by parity patterns of influence. Conversely, in cities in which there are high degrees of conflict around the Model Cities Program and low degrees of political integration, the chief executives are more inclined to shy away from the program. This type of sociopolitical environment is most often characterized by resident-dominant patterns of influence.

Quality of Agency Participation in Planning: While there is no clear linear relationship between patterns of influence and the quality of agency participation in planning, cities with parity citizen influence had a much greater proportion of high ratings on quality of agency participation than others, as can be noted in table 6-5. Fifty percent of these cities were rated excellent on agency participation in planning compared to only 22 percent of staff-dominant cities and 29 percent of resident-dominant cities. On the other end of the scale, 50 percent of staff-dominant cities were given poor ratings on this measure compared to 18.8 percent each for parity and resident-dominant cities.

We might conclude from these findings that the tendency in staff-dominant cities was to involve neither the residents nor the agencies in planning; in resident-dominant cities there was, by definition, a high degree of resident involvement but, as we noted in chapter 5, excessive degrees of citizen influence were associated with poor outcomes in other elements of the chain of planning objectives (planning products, plan implementation, and program performance). These effects of resident-dominant systems may be explained, in part, by the poorer quality of agency participation in planning that occurred

Table 6-5.   Patterns of Influence and Quality of Agency Participation in Planning

Quality of Agency Participation In Planning	Patterns of Influence		
	Staff Dominant (percent)	Parity (percent)	Resident Dominant (percent)
Poor	50	18.8	18.8
Fair	27.3	31.2	52.2
Excellent	22.7	50	29
Total	100	100	100
	(n=69)	(n=32)	(n=22)
(gamma -.065)			

in these cities (by comparison to parity cities). It does not, of course, explain poorer outcomes entirely. Staff-dominant cities received higher proportions of "poor" ratings on agency participation than other cities, and yet they appear more likely to do better than resident-dominant cities on the other outcome measures. Apparently, the generally poor performance regarding participation of residents and agencies in staff-dominant cities is associated with their having a lower capacity to achieve successful outcomes than parity cities. However, they seem to avoid some of the hazards in planning encountered by the resident-dominant cities.

Numbers of Agencies Participating in Planning: The low-negative association between patterns of influence and numbers of agencies participating in planning (gamma -.154) indicates that cities in which there were higher degrees of citizen influence were somewhat more likely to have fewer agencies participating in planning than other cities. For example: 38 percent of staff-dominant cities had high numbers of agencies participating; 32 percent of parity cities had high numbers of agencies participating; and 20 percent of resident-dominant cities had high numbers of agencies participating. While the differences in percentages between types of cities is not especially large, what is most significant is that a larger proportion of staff-dominant cities than others should report engaging large numbers of agencies in planning. That is, as previously indicated, staff-dominant cities were more likely than others to receive low ratings on *quality* of agency participation. Apparently, quantity is not a very good predictor of quality. This is borne out by the fact that, as we noted in chapter 5, staff-dominant cities did not achieve very high ratings on the other outcome variables. As will become apparent in the next sections when we examine the relationships of interorganizational factors to other elements in the chain of planning objectives, success at engaging large numbers of agencies in planning and implementation of programs has some dysfunctional consequences.

Planning Products

The impact of interorganizational field variables on selected qualities of the Comprehensive Demonstration Plan (CDP) is summarized in the relationships reported in table 6-6. Here, the positive influences of strong chief executive commitment and a high degree of agency participation in planning on planning products are quite evident; the negative effects of engaging large numbers of agencies in planning are also evident.

Chief Executive Commitment: There is a very strong-positive correlation between quality of the CDP and chief executive commitment (gamma .702). CDPs in cities where chief executives had strong commitments were rated "best" fifteen times as frequently as they were rated "worst." This ratio is twenty-seven times as great as for cities in which chief executive commitment was weak, and almost eleven times as great as those in which chief executive commitment was moderate. Along with this there is a substantial-positive correlation between chief executive commitment and percent categorical funds in the CDP (gamma .534) and a moderate-positive correlation between chief executive commitment and percent local funds in the CDP (gamma .395). These data affirm the general hypothesis stated in chapter 2 regarding the significance of the chief executive's support in attaining successful outcomes to planning. The findings also suggest that one of the most significant impacts of chief executive support during the planning period is in assembling resources and securing commitments of funds from agencies in the interorganizational field.

Table 6-6. Associations Between Interorganizational Field Variables and Planning Products (Gammas)

| Planning Products | Interorganizational Field Variables | | |
	Chief Executive Commitment	Quality of Agency Participation In Planning	Number of Agencies Participating In Planning
"Best/Worst" CDPs	.702	.748	−.065
Percent of Categorical Funds in the CDP	.534	.192	.106
Percent Local Funds in the CDP	.395	.003	−.111
Number of Agencies in the CDP	−.196	−.006	.712

The association between chief executive commitment and number of agencies included in the CDP is low-negative (gamma -.196). Thus, while strong chief executive support was positively related to acquisition of categorical funds and quality of the CDP, it did not have much of a bearing on agency numbers per se.

Quality of Agency Participation in Planning: While the relationships are not as impressive as those found for chief executive commitment, quality of agency participation in planning is positively associated with most planning products. As with chief executive commitment, the association between quality of agency participation in planning and the "best/worst" CDP rating is a very strong-positive one (gamma .748). The proportion of "best to worst" CDPs is four times as high for those cities in which quality of agency participation in planning was rated "excellent" as for those cities where quality was rated "fair," and almost twelve times as high as for cities where quality was rated "poor." Similarly, there is a low-positive association between quality of participation and percent of categorical funds in the CDP (gamma .192) and a negligible-positive association between quality of participation and percent local funds (gamma .003). The association between quality of agency participation in planning and numbers of agencies in the CDP is also negligible-negative (gamma -.006).

Number of Agencies in Planning: The general finding on this variable is that the larger the number of agencies in planning the weaker the outcomes on most planning products. The association between number of agencies participating in planning and quality of the CDP is negligible-negative (gamma -.065). Proportion of "best to worst" CDPs is lower for cities that had high numbers of agencies participating in planning, than for cities with low numbers of agencies participating. There is a low-positive association between numbers of agencies in planning and percent categorical funds in the CDP (gamma .106) and a low negative association between numbers of agencies in planning and percent local funds in CDP (gamma -.111). As expected, there is a strong-positive correlation between number of agencies in planning and number of agencies in the CDP (gamma .712).

Plan Implementation

While degree of chief executive commitment appears to be the variable that is most strongly related to good planning products, it is quality of agency participation in planning that seems to be most significant in regard to plan implementation (table 6-7). The negative effects of number of agencies in planning appear to persist into plan implementation.

Chief Executive Commitment: There is a negligible-positive association between chief executive commitment and implementation of citizen participation (gamma .019) reflecting our earlier description of the association between chief executive commitment and patterns of influence.

There is a low-positive relationship between chief executive commitment and implementation or coordination (gamma .214). Though this relationship is not as strong or as conclusive as we would have anticipated from the literature, the association is in the expected direction.

Quality of Agency Participation in Planning: The associations between quality of agency participation in planning and the plan implementation measures are both positive, the first substantial (gamma .677) and the second moderate (gamma .319). That these associations are stronger than those found in relation to chief executive commitment can be attributed, we think, to the fact that implementation is largely an agency function, whereas the mobilization of resources (whereby chief executive commitment proved to be most important) is largely an executive function.

Number of Agencies Participating in Planning: The number of agencies participating in planning has a low-negative association (gamma -.229) and a moderate-negative association (gamma -.361) with the two plan implementation variables. Thus, the negative effects of involving large numbers of agencies in planning appears to carry through from the planning process, to planning products, to plan implementation.

Table 6-7. Associations Between Interorganizational Field Variables and Plan Implementation Variables (Gammas)

| | Interorganizational Field Variables | | |
Plan Implementation Variables	Chief Executive Commitment	Quality of Agency Participation In Planning	Number of Agencies Participating In Planning
Implementation of Citizen Participation	.019	.677	−.229
Implementation of Coordination	.214	.319	−.361

Program Performance

Measures of program performance are consistent with other findings regarding relationships between interorganizational variables and elements in the chain of planning objectives. Chief executive commitment and quality of agency participation in planning are positively associated with the program performance measures. The associations between number of agencies in planning and program performance measures are, generally, negligible and negative. These findings are summarized in table 6-8 and will be discussed below.

Chief Executive Commitment: The association between spending of supplemental funds and chief executive commitment is negligible-positive for the first six months of the first year of program implementation (gamma .096). As indicated earlier, implementation of service delivery as reflected in the spending performance of the cities seemed to improve over time, and the cities were generally better at spending for the second six months than for the first six months. This occurs, in part, because federal granting agencies tend to be sensitive about the prompt expenditure of funds within the fiscal year for which they are granted. And this was especially true for Model Cities. Federal officials who must go before Congress to request authorization of funds to solve the cities' problems do not relish explaining why cities could not spend the funds granted for the first action year, particularly after so much effort, time, and money has been spent by the cities on planning their requests for funds. Thus, although "spending the money" was not an explicit objective of the Model Cities Program, the production of concrete results and service delivery required the expenditure of substantial proportions of the cities' grants. The increased spending pattern for the second six

Table 6-8. Associations Between Interorganizational Field Variables and Program Performance Variables (Gammas)

| Program Performance Variables | *Interorganizational Field Variables* | | |
	Chief Executive Commitment	*Quality of Agency Participation In Planning*	*Number of Agencies Participating In Planning*
Spending			
Six months	.096	.175	.086
Twelve months	.455	.299	−.079
Per Capita MNH at twelve months	.789	.302	−.085
"Most/Least" Successful Programs	.629	.700	.093

months of the program probably reflects, in part, pressures by HUD to increase rates of spending.

When HUD's concerns over the high rates of underspending experienced in the first six months of the program year were conveyed to the Model Cities, we might assume that the same political pressure exercised by the local chief executive to help secure categorical funds was available and used to push for rapid program development and expanded service delivery. And, indeed, this seems to have been the case. For the first six-month period there is no relationship between chief executive commitment and spending. But over the next six months, as HUD put pressure on the cities to implement programs more rapidly, we find a moderate-positive association between chief executive commitment and spending (gamma .455). The first program year per capita expenditures (of supplementary funds divided by the MNA population) at twelve months are even more strongly related to chief executive commitment (gamma .789). This is a potent demonstration of the impact of the chief executive's role on program implementation.

Finally, chief executive commitment is clearly associated with the extent to which first-year programs were rated as "most" or "least" succesful (gamma .629). Cities that had executives with "strong" commitment had a twelve-to-one ratio of "most" successful to "least" successful programs, approximately eighteen times and fourteen times as many respectively as cities with chief executives with "moderate" and "weak" commitments.

Quality of Agency Participation in Planning: The effects of quality of agency participation in planning are similar to those reported for the chief executive, though not as strong. The association between quality of agency participation and spending was low-positive at six months (gamma .175) and moderate-positive at twelve months (gamma .299), which reflects, we think, the same dynamics as operated with the chief executive. The association between per capita MNA spending at twelve months and quality of agency participation in planning is also moderate-positive (gamma .302).

The relationship between quality of agency participation in planning and quality of the first year program is very strong-positive (gamma .700). The ratio of "most" successful to ".least" successful programs was over eight to one for cities that had "excellent" participation of agencies in planning, which is more than eight times the proportion for cities in which agency participation was rated "fair," and twenty-four times the proportion for cities in which agency participation was rated "poor."

Number of Agencies Participating in Planning: The relationships between spending patterns and number of agencies involved in planning are negligible for all three spending measures (gammas .086, -.079, and -.085). The association between number of agencies in planning and quality of first-year program is negligible-positive (gamma .093). The actual distribution for this relationship shows that cities with the medium number of agencies participating in planning had the highest ratio of "most"-to-"least" successful programs (2.33).

SUMMARY

The findings presented in this chapter provide strong support for the proposition that *chief executive commitment and qualitative participation of agencies in planning enhanced the potential for successful planning outcomes* in the Model Cities Program. We qualified this proposition somewhat in respect to planning processes in noting that strong executive commitment and high quality of agency participation in planning were most closely associated with parity patterns of influence. In addition, the data indicate that strong executive leadership and high quality agency participation in planning are most likely to be found in sociopolitical environments characterized by low-to-moderate degrees of conflict and high degrees of political integration.

One question that remains to be dealt with in this discussion is: Why does a large number of agencies participating in planning appear to have a negligible or negative effect on all planning outcomes? At first thought, the number of agencies participating in the planning period would seem to reflect the extent to which the CDA actively responded to HUD's requirements for coordination of services. It might also reflect the extent to which the planning environment was conducive to agency involvement in the coordination efforts. The data in table 6-9 illustrate in some detail the unanticipated and rather important finding about the relationship between number of agencies participating in planning and planning outcomes that we have discussed in this chapter. In this instance we examine the relationship between number of agencies involved in planning and success of coordination. The data reveal a moderate *inverse* relationship between the number of agencies involved in the planning process and the implementation of coordination in the first program year.

The finding, that large numbers have a negative effect, can be most easily explained from a practical standpoint: it is relatively more difficult to plan and coordinate activities among many agencies than among few agencies. The meshing of complementary activities and

Table 6-9.   Number of Agencies Involved in the Planning Process and Degree of Success in Coordination

	Number of Agencies Involved In Planning		
Coordination Degree of Success	low (9 or fewer) (percent)	moderate (10-15) (percent)	high (16-33) (percent)
low	18.7	15.0	35.3
moderate	56.3	75.0	58.8
high	25.0	10.0	5.9
Total	100	100	100
(gamma -.367)	(n=16)	(n=20)	(n=17

other planning and coordinative tasks are more manageable when nine or fewer agencies are involved with the CDA than when sixteen-or-more agencies are involved. Indeed, it is questionable whether the planning and coordination of local services can be meaningfully accomplished when the planner must involve the number and scope of services described by HUD as components of a comprehensive approach (see p. 12).

With what range and mix of services can planning and coordination projects operate most effectively? The Model Cities findings suggest that, in terms of numbers, the optimum range of agencies involved in planning is nine or less. But numbers alone may not explain the entire story. It would be helpful to understand why communities that were operating under the same set of HUD guidelines and requirements involved different numbers of agencies in planning. One explanation would be that city size affects the numbers of agencies available (for example, large cities would have a larger pool of potential agencies to recruit for the planning and coordination effort than small cities). However, as we shall indicate in the next chapter, the associations between city size and products and performance in planning are negative.

Assuming that equal efforts were devoted to gaining not just participation, but substantive agency commitments to the coordination effort, we might expect to find a positive association between the number of agencies participating in planning and the percent of categorical funds in the CDP budget. That is, the greater the number of agencies participating, the more categorical funds that would be potentially available for commitment. However, the data reveal that this relationship is rather weak (gamma .106, see table 6-6). Communities with the *fewest* agencies involved in the planning process obtained proportionately almost as much categorical money as those with the largest number of agencies.[a] Thus, there appears to be a discrepancy between the quantity of commitments obtained in different communities, as reflected in the number of agencies participating in planning, and the quality of these commitments as reflected in the amount of funds that participating agencies agreed to contribute to these planning arrangements.

In sum, it is not clear that the inverse relationship found between the number of agencies participating in planning and the success of the planning and coordination effort should be interpreted strictly as a function of the comparatively greater difficulty attributable to coordinating large numbers of participants. At the very least, the unanticipated finding that the number of agencies involved in planning had little impact upon the percent of categorical funds committed to the program must be taken into account. This suggests that, in addition to a numerical count of agency participation, we must assess the *quality* of agency commitments to the planning effort.

Between the planning period and the first program year the number of participating agencies decreased. As noted in table 6-2, a substantial number of agencies did not participate beyond the planning period. Although, in general, there were fewer agencies participating in the program year than in the planning period, we still find a moderate negative association (gamma -.378) between the number of agencies involved in the CDP and implementation of coordination. According to these data, projects in which less than a dozen agencies were involved were more likely to achieve positive results than those in which there were a larger number of agencies. These data support Bolan's observation:

> If carrying out the proposal involves a great deal of coordination among a large number of autonomous and dispersed groups, it is more likely to be resisted and eventually rejected (largely because of uncertainty that it will actually be carried out as proposed). Even if adopted, it may easily be subverted in implementation. Proposals that concentrate action within a single agency or a relatively few individuals and involve few external coordination problems will more likely be adopted.[1]

We have found no empirical references in the literature regarding the question of how the numbers of agencies that participate in planning efforts affect outcomes. However, there is a body of research on group dynamics that is relevant to this question because planning ef-

[a]We should note that the supplemental funds in CDP budgets (against which the percent of categorical funds was calculated) were allocated on a formula basis that was unrelated to the number of participating agencies.

forts are conducted, in large part, through the work of small groups—the task forces or committees composed of representatives of participating agencies. Some of the findings here are suggestive. For example, Thomas notes, in a study of welfare departments, that units composed of small numbers of workers achieved greater role consensus than units composed of larger numbers.[2] (While the numbers of workers in sections of welfare departments are different units of analysis than numbers of agencies in planning projects, the problems of interaction of different numbers of task group members are similar in both cases.)

In another research effort, Hare found that as the size of discussion groups increased, the degree of consensus decreased; members were more dissatisfied with the discussion; and there was a tendency for the larger groups to break into factions.[3] These findings point to some of the difficulties that may have been encountered in the work of Model Cities Program committees that contained representatives of numerous agencies.

Our findings in Model Cities, of course, do not suggest that numbers of agencies larger than nine magically assure the failure of planning efforts. Rather, the finding underscores a general fact of which planners are aware but which has not received much explicit attention in studies of planning or in the policy guidelines for planning projects. Namely, *at some point* numbers make a difference: social and physical arrangements for meetings may become burdensome; informal communications may become difficult to sustain.

NOTES

1. Richard S. Bolan, "Community Decision Behavior: The Culture of Planning," *Journal of the American Institute of Planners* 35, no. 5 (September 1969): 307.

2. Edwin J. Thomas, "Role Conceptions and Organizational Size," *American Sociological Review* 20, no. 1 (February 1959): 30-47.

3. A. Paul Hare, "Interaction and Consensus in Different Sized Groups," *Group Dynamics: Research and Theory*, eds. Dorwin Cartwright and Alvin Zander (Evanston, Ill.: Row, Peterson and Co., 1953), pp. 507-18.

✳ Chapter 7

The Community Context

Up to this point in the analysis we have dealt with the composition of the planning systems in Model Cities (resident participants and professionals) and the interorganizational field (the agencies involved in the coordination effort and the behavior of the cities' chief executives), studying variables that were directly relevant to Model Cities Program developments. This chapter examines the somewhat more remote contextual factors related to the various elements in HUD's chain of planning objectives. The major contextual factors are: city population size; extent of the cities' planning experience based on an index that combined length of experience in both urban renewal and public housing program development; and the cities' per capita expenditures (total city budget divided by total population of the city).

There are some significant differences between these contextual variables and the variables we dealt with earlier. First, it is not our intent to search for direct relationships between these global contextual variables and Model Cities outcomes. Clearly, intervening variables must be considered in order to account for relationships that might exist, for example, between population size and citizen influence, or between planning experience and degree of success in coordination.

Second, these contextual variables are, by comparison to the action system and interorganization field variables, less dynamic in regard to the planning process because, from a time perspective, they clearly precede the planning experience and, unlike the other variables, these contextual factors are hardly affected by the planning experience during the period under study.

Finally, the contextual variables are not as easily changeable by policy and practice as the other variables. For example, degree of citizen influence and planners' role behaviors are elements in planning that may be altered by changes in policy and practice. By comparison, city size, planning experience, and per capita expenditures are not subject to the influence of programs over a short period of time.

However, even though these variables have a relatively global, static, and fixed quality, there is a practical use in studying them. As antecedant variables they help to explain and qualify some of the relationships discussed in preceding chapters. This can be illustrated by the example of the relationship between city size and degree of success in coordination. While it would be difficult for a planner to alter the size of the city in which he is working, and certainly it would be extremely difficult to do it within the time period covered by this study, it is still useful to the planner to know that medium-size cities (population 50,000 to 249,000) are more likely to do better in coordination efforts than other cities. This finding, we believe, cannot be explained by size per se. Rather, this association occurs because cities of medium size are large enough to contain a substantial number and variety of service agencies as well as a sufficiently large pool of skilled and experienced professional personnel who can develop and implement coordination plans. Yet these cities are small enough to allow for development of a network of informal relationships among the various city agencies, and between the city agencies and the city government, to facilitate the implementation of coordination efforts. By comparison, small cities (49,000 and under), which may have a network of informal relationships, usually do not command the required level of agency resources and staff skills. And the very large cities (over 249,999) may have an abundance of agency resources and professional personnel, but the network among agencies and between agencies and government required for planning is difficult to establish in these cities because there are more layers of bureaucracy. Accordingly, it would follow that with regard to community size, obstacles to service coordination efforts are more likely in both very large and very small communities than in middle-size communities.[1]

What practical use can planners make of this finding? Let us consider the smaller cities. Small communities cannot afford to support many full-time professional employees; many professionals prefer to work in larger, more cosmopolitan communities and, therefore, the smaller community often finds it difficult to attract skilled and seasoned professionals. One way of increasing the pool of expertise is by engaging professional consultants. Most professional consulting work is done by private consulting firms;[a] a small part of it is done by academics from colleges and universities.

One problem that the community with insufficient professional expertise will face in using professional consultants is that the political and professional leaders of the community are more likely to be both insecure and uninformed in their dealings with professional consultants and, therefore, less likely to establish appropriate contracts with them.

Federal agencies could provide more assistance to small communities in dealing with these kinds of relationships by providing guidelines for selection of firms, model contracts, referral services, and advice to local governments in their dealings with consulting firms.

Planners in large cities would make different use of the finding about the relationship between city size and degree of coordination success. For example, the effects of the complexity of organizational relationships in large cities can be reduced by limiting the size and scope of the coordination effort. Here we can make brief use of some findings on the interorganizational field discussed in chapter 6. Our data showed that degree of success in coordination is related *negatively* to the numbers of agencies engaged in planning and implementing the coordination project: the greater the number of agencies, the less the likelihood of success. Large cities usually contain more agencies than small cities; hence the greater potential of large cities to engage more participating agencies than small cities. Planners in large cities might, therefore, make special efforts to limit the numbers of agencies participating in coordination projects.

Finally, city size is positively related to the degree of autonomy of the residents' organization (pp. 74-75). At the same time, extreme degrees of resident-organization staff autonomy were found to be *negatively* associated with success of coordination, and cities in which there were intermediate degrees of resident-organization staff autonomy were the most likely to have successful coordination outcomes. Of course, the large cities contain many subpopulations that form special interest groups based on shared characteristics such as race, class, and neighborhood; these groups are more inclined than residents' groups in smaller and more homogeneous communities to claim autonomy. In the long run, the benefits of extreme degrees of

[a]Approximately 70 percent of the Model Cities made use of professional consulting firms. A somewhat larger proportion of small cities made use of them than other cities.

autonomy for consumers' organizations appear to be dubious, whereas the benefits of consumer organizations having intermediate degrees of autonomy are considerably higher. Therefore, planners in large cities might make special efforts to maximize citizen influence in planning by encouraging resident participation *within the established institutional structure.*

Before moving to more detailed analysis of contextual variables, it should be noted that there are moderate-to-strong-positive-degrees of association among the three contextual variables used in this analysis (table 7-1). The strongest association is between size and planning experience (gamma .725) and the weakest is between per capita expenditures and city population size (gamma .297). Larger cities are likely to have had more planning experience than other cities; and large cities and cities with more planning experience tend to have higher per capita expenditures than others.

We studied other contextual variables but did not include them. For example, while regional variations existed among the Model Cities, we thought this factor too remote from the local experience to have practical use in analyzing the dynamics of locality planning. Moreover, although there were differences among the regions, the other contextual variables we discuss (size, experience, per capita expenditures) generally operate in the same way *within* each of the regions as they do in the entire population of cities.[2] Also we examined race and degree of turbulence in the cities. However, we found that both of these variables were strongly associated with race and conflict in the MNAs as they are discussed in chapter 4, and the contextual analysis of them on a citywide basis added little more.

In the following discussion we follow an analytic framework similar to that used in the two preceding chapters. The variables presented here have been previously defined except for planning experience, which will be described in the analysis below. As shown in figure 7-1 we will analyze the ways in which the three contextual variables are associated with the different elements in the chain of planning objectives.

Table 7-1. Associations Between Three Contextual Factors (Gammas)

	City Planning Experience	City Per Capita Expenditures
City Population Size	.725	.297
City Planning Experience	—	.498

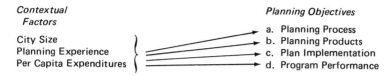

Figure 7-1. Relationships Between Contextual Factors and Planning Objectives

CONTEXTUAL FACTORS AND THE PLANNING PROCESS

There is a moderate-positive degree of association between each of the three contextual variables and patterns of influence that developed in planning (table 7-2). That is, large cities with several years of planning experience and high per capita budgets were more likely than others to develop planning systems with high degrees of citizen influence.

Taking a closer look at the relationship between city size and patterns of influence, the data in table 7-3 reveal that medium-size cities were proportionately more than three times as likely to have strong citizen influence as small cities, and that large cities were proportionately more than five times as likely as small cities to achieve this result. And whereas 70.3 percent of small cities were judged to have weak citizen influence, only 41 percent of the large cities reflected this pattern of participation.

This relationship is somewhat strengthened (gamma .445) when the data are collapsed into categories that fit the operational definitions of small cities (less than 250,000) and large cities (more than 250,000) employed by Yin et al.[3] Using these two categories of city size, it can be seen in table 7-4 that large cities achieved strong citizen influence proportionately more than twice as often as small cities. And while 62.2 percent of the small cities had weak citizen influence, this pattern of participation occurred in only 40.9 percent of the large cities. While these results disagree with the findings of Yin et al. and a study by HUD, they correspond with Austin's analysis of city size and citizen participation in the antipoverty program.[4]

Finding a relationship between citizen influence and a demographic characteristic such as city size, of course, says nothing about why the relationship exists. Clearly, citizen participation is not directly a function of such a global property as city size. Other research on community behavior suggests many possible variables with which city size is associated that might account for this relationship (pp. 68-70).

Table 7-2. Associations Between Contextual Factors and Elements in the Planning Process (Gammas)

	Contextual Factors		
	City Size	City Planning Experience	Citywide Per Capita Expenditures
Patterns of Influence	.363	.336	.301

Table 7-3. City Size and Patterns of Influence

	City Size		
Patterns of Influence	*Small (49,999 and under)*	*Medium (50,000- 249,999)*	*Large (250,000 and over)*
Staff Dominant	70.3	57.4	41.0
Parity	24.3	24.6	29.5
Resident Dominant	5.4	18.0	29.5
Total	100	100	100
	(n=37)	(n=61)	(n=44)
(gamma .363)			

Table 7-4. Patterns of Influence in Small and Large Cities

	City Size	
Patterns of Influence	*Small (under 250,000)*	*Large (250,000+)*
Staff Dominant	62.2	40.9
Parity	24.5	29.6
Resident Dominant	13.3	29.6
Total	100	100.1[a]
	(n=98)	(n=44)
(gamma .445)		

[a]Due to rounding

As noted in chapter 2, studies by Aiken and Alford suggest that in large cities there will be greater experience and expertise to apply to the implementation of new policies than in small cities; and that a smaller proportion of the overall system will be required to obtain a "critical mass" of support for policy implementation in large cities than in small cities.[5] Applying this theoretical view, one possible explanation for the relationship between size and citizen influence in Model Cities is that large cities had greater access to professional experience, knowledge, and skill for the implementation of HUD policy, and that access encouraged moderate-to-strong citizen influence during the first years of the program.[6] If this were the case, we would then expect that the variables of professional experience, knowledge, and skill, if held constant, would suppress the relationship between city size and citizen influence.

One approach to measuring these variables is to assume that the *length* of a city's experience in a related program area, such as urban renewal, will reflect the city's development of knowledge, skill, and other relevant characteristics that are prerequisites for implementing Model Cities policy. That is, "professional experience" may be inferred from the length of time that a city has been operating a related program; the earlier the city submitted an acceptable application for that program, the more time it has had to learn from and integrate its experience. We do not mean to suggest that urban renewal programs were distinguished for encouraging active citizen participation. There is much evidence to the contrary.[7] Rather, the assumption is that, over time, cities engaged in urban renewal activities attract and cultivate a pool of professionals who are skilled in community planning. This skill may be used to undermine and deflate citizen participation or to encourage and nurture it, depending on the values operative in the planning system. Given appropriate incentives from HUD, it can be expected that these skills would be turned to the task of encouraging citizen participation.

On the basis of these assumptions, we used the length of experience in urban renewal as an indicator of the variable of professional experience-knowledge-skill and introduced this variable into our analysis of city size and citizen influence. Consistent with the Aiken and Alford position, as already noted, large cities were more likely to have a greater amount of experience in urban renewal programs than small cities. Examining the relationship between city size and citizen influence, holding length of urban renewal experience constant, we found that the relationship between city size and citizen influence was suppressed in cities that had the most experience in urban renewal (gamma .005). As shown in table 7-5, *population size had little bearing on the degree of citizen influence that developed in the Model Cities Programs for those cities where previous experience in urban renewal was greatest. However, for cities with moderate or little past experience, a positive relationship between city size and citizen influence remained* (gamma .427 and .364, respectively).[8] These results lend weight to the view that relevant knowledge and skills gained through experience are one of the intervening factors that partially explain the relationship between size and citizen influence. At the same time, it appears that other variables associated with city size may be operative.

Table 7-5. City Size and Patterns of Influence for Cities with Different Degrees of Urban Renewal Experience (Percent)

Patterns of Influence	Least Experience[a]			Moderate Experience[b]			Most Experience[c]		
	Small	Medium	Large	Small	Medium	Large	Small	Medium	Large
Staff Dominant	84.2	60.0	71.4	66.7	61.9	28.6	0.0	44.4	33.3
Parity	15.8	20.0	14.3	16.7	33.3	28.6	66.7	22.2	33.3
Resident Dominant	0.0	20.0	14.3	16.7	4.8	42.9	33.3	33.3	33.3
Total	100	100	100	100.1[d]	100	100.1[d]	100	99.9[d]	99.9[d]
	(n=19)	(n=15)	(n=7)	(n=6)	(n=21)	(n=7)	(n=3)	(n=27)	(n=27)

[a]gamma .364
[b]gamma .427
[c]gamma .005
[d]due to rounding

**Per Capita Expenditures and
Citizen Influence**

The positive association between per capita expenditures and citizen influence (gamma .301) is accounted for, in part, by the strong-positive association between per capita expenditures and planning experience (gamma .498). That is, cities with greater planning experience are more likely to have large per capita expenditures than other cities. As pointed out in the preceding discussion, cities with more planning experience are also more likely than others to have higher degrees of citizen influence in planning (gamma .336). An additional factor that would explain the positive association between per capita expenditures and citizen influence is the financial costs of citizen participation. As Frej and Specht note, to encourage and maintain citizen participation in urban areas is often a costly proposition. Cities that have larger per capita budgets are in a better position to foster high degrees of citizen influence than other cities.[9]

In sum, the data on the Model Cities experience suggest that strong citizen participation is most likely to occur in well-populated cities. It also appears that the accumulated knowledge and skill that come from a city's experience in operating related community planning programs carry over to the development of citizen participation, particularly in small and moderate-size cities. Planning experience is also associated positively with per capita expenditures, which in turn is associated with degree of citizen influence in planning.

RELATIONSHIPS TO OTHER PLANNING OBJECTIVES

While there are consistently positive associations between planning process objectives and contextual factors, the picture changes when we go on to consider the other outcomes in the chain of planning objectives. That is, the factors of city size, city planning experience, and per capita city budget show from weak to moderate positive associations with implementation of citizen participation, negligble relationships with the quality of the CDP, and uniformly negative associations with program performance as measured by spending.

One explanation for these varied findings is that the positive relationships between size, experience, per capita budget, and the implementation of citizen participation in the program year reflect the fact that the larger, wealthier, and more experienced cities were more likely than others to have developed resident-dominant patterns of influence during the planning period; and while cities with resident-dominant patterns of influence tended to score high on implementation of citizen participation, they were distinguished neither for the quality of their CDPs nor for their performance on program spending. This explanation suggests that contextual factors may have the greatest bearing on process objectives, which in turn go on to influence other outcomes in the chain of objectives. These relationships among outcomes on the different Model Cities objectives will be explored in greater depth in the next chapter.

NOTES

1. For a more detailed analysis of these findings see, Neil Gilbert and Harry Specht, *Coordinating Social Services: An Analysis of Community, Organizational and Staff Characteristics* (New York: Praeger Publications, Inc., 1977).

2. Ibid., pp. 36-39.

3. Robert K. Yin et al., *Citizen Organization: Increasing Client Control over Services* (Santa Monica, Calif.: RAND Corp., 1973), pp. 50-51.

4. Department of Housing and Urban Development, *The Model Cities Program: A Comparative Analysis of the Planning Process in Eleven Cities* (Washington, D.C.: Government Printing Office, 1970), pp. 22-23; Yin, et al.; David Austin, "Resident Participation: Political Mobilization and Organizational Co-optation" *Public Administration Review* 32 (Sept. 1972): 409-420.

5. Michael Aiken and Robert Alford, "Community Structure and Innovation: The Case of Urban Renewal," *American Sociological Review* 35 (August 1970): 650-65.

6. While there appeared to be some disagreements within HUD about the degree of citizen influence that was desirable during the early years of Model Cities, the balance of power rested with the HUD advocates of moderate-to-strong influence for citizen groups. We analyze how selection of participating cities was used to support the policy of active citizen participation in chapter 9. After the Nixon administration came to office the emphasis on active citizen participation was considerably diminished.

7. See, for example, Scott Greer, *Urban Renewal and American Cities* (Indianapolis: Bobbs-Merrill Co., 1965); Peter Rossi and Robert Dentler, *The Politics of Urban Renewal* (New York: Free Press, 1961), pp. 287-88; James Q. Wilson, "Planning and Politics: Citizen Participation in Urban Renewal," in *Urban Renewal: People, Politics, and Planning*, eds. Jewel Bellush and Murray Hausknecht (New York: Anchor Books, 1967), pp. 287-301.

8. The same pattern of findings occurred when we examined the relationship between target area size and citizen influence, holding the city's experience in urban renewal constant.

9. William Frej and Harry Specht, "The Housing and Community Development Act of 1974: Implications for Policy and Planning," *Social Service Review* 60 (June 1976): 286-89.

✳ **Part III**

**Outcomes, Predictions,
and Applications**

✳ Chapter 8

Outcomes: The Congruence of
Planning Objectives

In the preceding chapters we analyzed the relationships among elements in the community context, the planning system, the interorganizational field, and a series of program objectives. These objectives were described as a paradigm—links in a cumulative chain consisting of: (1) a planning process involving a strong element of citizen influence that leads to the development of; (2) a high quality Comprehensive Demonstration Plan (CDP) containing clearly stated and innovative policies derived from rational analysis to guide; (3) a process of program implementation involving a high degree of coordination of services and citizen participation, leading to; (4) a high quality of performance in establishing programs aimed at improving the quality of life in urban communities. The assumption underlying this paradigm is that the objectives are connected in a positive and reinforcing manner so that achievement of objective 1 strengthens the likelihood that a city will achieve objective 2 and so forth.

In focusing upon the outcomes of Model Cities our purpose in this chapter is to assess the extent to which the links in HUD's chain of planning objectives were actually connected as described in the above paradigm. We are not seeking to evaluate the overall Model Cities outcomes against ideal standards of success. For example, when considering the quality of the CDP our primary concern is not how many of the plans were exceptional or of "best quality" but, rather, to what extent the achievement of this objective was associated with the achievement of other objectives. Here the question is whether the degree of quality of the plans produced by the Model Cities bears any relationship to degree of success in program implementation.

The chain of planning objectives paradigm implies that there is an orderly progression in planning; it seems natural to assume that a rational, technically sound plan is a requisite for successful program implementation. Yet, on reflection, many planners can cite cases of technically excellent and imaginative plans that were left to collect dust on agency shelves while less estimable designs received support for implementation.[1] The assumption that there is a direct positive relationship among the various Model Cities objectives is *theoretically* plausible, but it is without substantial empirical verification from other community planning experiences. And if one considers the question theoretically, the argument can be made that some of the objectives in the chain of planning objectives have only a tenuous relationship to others; and some objectives are unrelated and may even be in conflict with each other. As we examine the extent to which the cities' relative achievements on different outcome measures are congruent with the chain of planning objectives model, we will consider the case for potential conflicts and the absence of connections between links in this chain.

PLANNING PROCESS
AND RELATED OUTCOMES

One of the immediate objectives in Model Cities was to create a structure and process for community planning that involved MNA residents in more than an advisory or rubber-stamp capacity. Presumably, citizen input in the decision-making process would improve the quality of the CDP and of the program. But HUD required that the CDP be a rational, comprehensive, and technically sophisticated document. Conducting surveys, preparing analyses of census data, budgeting, and developing five-year projections are exercises that, by temperament and training, professional planners are well equipped to handle. The layman is usually neither familar with these techniques nor enthusiastic about the prospects of investing the time and energy required to master them. After all, that is what professionals are paid to do. What then does the citizen offer to warrant the assumption that his involvement will improve the planning product that HUD required?

One answer is that citizens who have lived with and experienced the problems of their communities are in the best position to recognize and understand these problems; they can "tell it like it really is." From this perspective, "the supposedly hard, cold data of professional planners would be modified by the direct visceral experiences of low-income neighborhood residents."[2] In this view, the "real life experiences" of the poor rather than the supposedly impersonal and unfeeling abstractions of professionals can provide an optimum guide to neighborhood planning. As Bloomberg and Rosenstock explain, one of the reasons given for resident participation in planning is that residents "can contribute much from their own experience to the formulation of programs and projects to alleviate and reduce poverty."[3]

A similar view is expressed in HUD's explanation of the specific assumptions upon which performance standards for citizen involvement in the Model Cities Program were based:

> The best intentioned officials and technicians are often, by their training, experience, and life styles, unfamiliar with or even insensitive to the problems and aspirations of model neighborhood residents; therefore, resident ideas and priorities can result in more relevant, sensitive, and effective plans and programs.[4]

However, various studies of low-income neighborhood residents' perceptions of local conditions raise serious doubts about this explanation of the relationship between citizen participation in planning and the quality of planning products. For example, Gilbert and Eaton, in a survey of over six thousand residents in eight of Pittsburgh's antipoverty program neighborhoods found that the majority of residents viewed neighborhood conditions with greater equanimity than the professional and political leaders of the community. Most of the residents expressed satisfaction with neighborhood conditions, while a larger proportion of professional planners rated them as inadequate on the basis of much supportive data available to them.[5] Similarly, Grosser found that professionals were considerably more critical of neighborhood conditions on New York's Lower East Side than were the community residents.[6]

More generally, there is another side to the assertion that those who have lived in low-income communities and who have experienced their problems have a special insight into the situation that can enhance planning efforts. That is, *people adjust where possible.* For a variety of reasons, residents of low-income neighborhoods may be less objective in assessing their circumstances than professional planners. As Lippitt et al. explain:

> It is worth noting some of the reasons for ignorance and distortion of the self-image of an individual and in the ideas which members of a group, or-

ganization, or community share about the system to which they belong. If the system is currently in pain or trouble, this in itself may generate defensive obstacles to accurate self-diagnosis.... Both individuals and groups may be afflicted by a motivated inability to see their own shortcomings, whether they be simple disabilities or complex expressions of hostility and destructiveness.[7]

Of course, it might be argued that citizen influence in decision making introduces an element of social choice into the planning process and that the particular skill and special insider's knowledge of local conditions is only incidental or nonexistent. The introduction of value judgments and social choices into the planning process considerably changes the basis for evaluating citizen input. If we adopt the position that citizen participation is "good" *regardless* of the efficiency or effectiveness of the products of planning, then there is little point to measuring program outcomes. The appropriate measure of success with this reigning value is "citizen happiness with the process." (And some theoreticians hold that the higher the degree of citizen participation in planning, the greater the degree of *dissatisfaction* with planning outcomes.[8]) The problem with the position that participation is "good" regardless of economy or effectiveness in the Model Cities context is that HUD was quite concerned about program outcomes. In addition to citizen participation, HUD's planning model also emphasized the comprehensive, rational decision-making approach to planning.

Theoretically, this approach is oriented more toward the professional and technical expertise dimensions of planning than toward the sociopolitical. In the rational decision-making approach, planning is conceived of as an orderly and logical progression from diagnosis to action based upon analysis of relevant facts and theories; the problem under consideration is diagnosed, solutions or ends (programmatic goals) are decided upon, programmatic means are designed to achieve the solution, and the effectiveness of these means is assessed. In this manner the logical or "best" solution is found. With this approach the major criterion of choice in planning is technical rationality rather than social acceptability.

The sociopolitical dimensions of planning are treated with greater prominence in the incremental approach to decision-making which seeks to achieve small remedial gains through a process of successive, limited comparisons between "what is" and "what is acceptable or feasible in the way of change."[9] Here the technical aspects of designing the "best" programmatic solution are deemphasized. Instead, the test of a "good" plan is the extent to which it captures the agreement of relevant interest groups. In the incremental approach, interactional tasks such as exchange, compromise, and development of agreement among competing interests and values are the predominant features of the planning process.

We are not arguing that citizen participation is entirely incompatible with comprehensive rational planning, but we are suggesting that it would seem more reasonable to anticipate a degree of conflict between the first two objectives (a planning process with strong citizen influence and the creation of a quality CDP judged mainly according to criteria of technical rationality) than to expect that these objectives would be mutually reinforcing.

Finally, it might be more sensible to make the case that active citizen involvement in planning is not as necessarily instrumental for the quality of planning products as it is for the implementation of plans. That is, citizen participation is necessary for implementation because, regardless of the design of the CDP, without citizen involvement the effectiveness of implementation suffers. The view here, in terms of HUD's chain of planning objectives, is that while the link between objective "1" and "2" may be tenuous or nonexistent, achievement of both "1" and "2" are *necessary* for successful implementation of planning objectives. But what degree of citizen influence in the planning process is required if such participation serves primarily the objective of paving the way to implementation rather than actually shaping plans? Applied to HUD's mandate for participation, the question is: To what extent is it necessary that participation to influence planning decisions be of more than an advisory type to satisfy this objective? A definitive answer to these questions cannot be given, but evidence from Rossi and Dentler's study of citizen participation in urban renewal suggests that commitment to implementation can be achieved through a passive form of citizen participation in which little policy-making influence is exercised in the development of the plan.

> Reviewing the successes and failures of the citizen participation activities of the Conference, it is clear that this organization made its greatest contribution in its passive rather than in its active roles. That is to say, the Conference obtained for the idea of planning and for the plan itself a mass base of support which facilitated the planning process and the acceptance of the Final Plan in the local community and "downtown." At the same time, however, the Conference was unable to modify the plan to conform in all details to the goals the Conference held out as desirable.[10]

Having raised a few questions about the extent to which strong citizen influence in planning is necessarily prerequisite to or consistent with other desired outcomes in HUD's chain of planning objectives, let us now turn to review the results in Model Cities. As summarized in table 8-1, six of the ten outcome measures show negative relationships to the degree of citizen influence in the planning process. The one substantial positive relationship (gamma .682) is found between citizen influence in planning and citizen participation in program implementation, which is to be expected. In general these findings appear to confirm at least some of the doubts expressed in the preceding discussion about the instrumental value of citizen influence in the planning process. That is, the findings suggest that there is a negative relationship between citizen influence in planning and the achievement of objectives related to the quality of the CDP and program performance. However, as noted in chapter 5, a closer examination of the data reveals that these doubts about the consequences of citizen influence are only partially confirmed. Staff-dominant patterns of influence in the planning process did not yield substantially more high-quality CDPs or a substantially better record on program performance than resident-dominant patterns. Rather, it was the parity patterns of influence that seemed to be most closely linked to the achievement of the other objectives. Thus, the weak statistical relationships reflect the fact that high levels of achievement on the various objectives occurred most frequently in cities on the midpoint of the resident-influence continuum. This is the case, too, in respect to the two instances where there are positive associations with citizen influence: implementation of coordination (gamma .357) and implementation of citizen participation (gamma .682). In both cases the positive association reflects the influence of a parity system more than it does the influence of a resident-dominant system (see tables 5-6 and 5-7).

Table 8-1. Assocations Between Patterns of Influence in the Planning Process and Other Model Cities Objectives (Gammas)

Other Objectives	Patterns of Influence
Outcome Measures of CDP Quality	
Percent of categorical funds in the CDP	.126
Percent of local funds in the CDP	−.161
Number of agencies in the CDP	−.116
Ratings of "best/worst" CDP	−.117
Outcome Measures of the Implementation Process	
Implementation of coordination	.357
Implementation of citizen participation	.682
Outcome Measures of Program Performance	
Percent of supplemental funds spent at six months	−.200
Percent of supplemental funds spent at twelve months	−.064
Per capita MNA spending at twelve months	.164
Ratings of "most/least" successful programs	−.222

These findings imply that, *if it is not overbearing,* citizen influence in planning is of instrumental value to other objectives. The findings do not, however, inform us as to precisely what it is about the parity pattern of influence that presumably facilitates the achievement of other objectives. Is it the blending of technical expertise with the values and knowledge of local residents? Or is it the commitments to implementation that are developed through meaningful citizen involvement in planning? The data do not answer these questions. We can only speculate that, perhaps, both of these factors played a role in the achievement record of parity cities. But as long as we have entered the realm of speculation, let us offer another explanation that transcends these factors.

It might be observed that these findings are merely a reaffirmation of the virtues of the "golden mean" between technocracy and democracy, or that they offer the well-worn advice that "moderation in all things is best." We believe that both observations are correct in a sense, but not necessarily in the literal sense that a moderate amount of citizen influence is instrumentally the "best" device for the achievement of other planning objectives. Rather it may be that a *general capacity* to achieve the "golden mean" requires a high degree of technical competence, patience, discipline, and reasonableness, as well as a sociopolitical climate in which these qualities can flourish. That this holds true for the community planning enterprise should be immediately obvious to anyone who has engaged in planning efforts that involve the creation of a planning structure and management of a planning process by which residents, agencies, and city hall communicate and exchange ideas around the design of policy.

Cooperation and trust among parties is essential to the development of parity planning arrangements, as is the tolerance of a certain amount of ambiguity concerning the locus of "final authority" and the quesitons of how and when it may be exercised. The sophisticated use of bargaining and negotiation, and the willingness to compromise before the brink are also important factors in sustaining parity arrangements. All of which is to say that to create and maintain workable planning arrangements requires a constellation of technical and sociopolitical skills and attitudes on the part of residents and professionals that are not characteristically found in staff-dominant and resident-dominant settings. Hence, the parity cities' high achievement scores on other objectives may be as much a reflection of planners and politicians who possess these skills and attitudes, and of the sociopolitical contexts in which they are located, as they are of the instrumental value of citizen influence per se. Theoretically, this explanation would account, at least in part, for the poor records of achievement under both citizen-dominant and staff-dominant planning arrangements.

In sum, to the extent that HUD's mandate for citizen participation in planning is defined more in terms of the parity than the staff-dominant or resident-dominant patterns, our findings reveal apparent connections between the first link and other desired outcomes in the chain of planning objectives.[11] However, it is indeterminate as to whether this relationship is traceable directly to the consequences of citizen influence or to other factors that accompany the development of parity patterns of influence.

PLANNING PRODUCTS AND RELATED OUTCOMES

Does the quality of the planning product make a difference with regard to implementation? No doubt HUD thought so, considering the time, money, and emphasis that was placed upon the preparation of CDPs compared to, for example, the virtually unstructured program packaging that preceded project funding in the antipoverty program.[12] However, we pose the question because, like art, a "good" plan reflects elegance, logic, wisdom, and imagination; but unlike art its value is not judged on aesthetic criteria. Plans must be valued by the extent to which they are implemented and the extent to which implementation produces desired consequences. In this regard the rationalist impulse supports the belief that "good" planning makes a difference. And the blending of the rationalist impulse with self-interest predisposes professional community planners to uphold this belief.

Nevertheless, there is a dearth of empirical evidence to confirm that the quality of the plan—or, for that matter, that *planning itself*— is related to degree of success in program implementation. The evidence that exists seems to point in the other direction. For example, in her study of city planning, Rabinovitz comments:

> "Wisdom" can be said to be present if a planner's program anticipates the problems, wants, and resources of the city involved and if it contains mechanisms sufficient to overcome the ecological forces driving the city along its current path. The planner must also be equipped to calculate correctly the outcome of the steps taken to alter this course. The participation of an expert and the existence of a planning agency do not insure such wisdom. Indeed, an enormous amount of effort is devoted each year in American cities to dealing with the unintended consequences of previous technical decisions.
>
> Even if experts have the requisite wisdom to manage development,

there is no guarantee that they will be able to influence its course. Urban governments have shown a tremendous capacity to ignore development pressures and the expert's advice. In one survey, the Urban Land Institute noted that while 102 of the 114 reporting cities had planning departments, only ten made specific reference to their plans.[13]

As for planning on a larger scale, at the national level, Wildavsky raises and answers the same questions that we ask about locality planning:

> Is there a single example of successful national economic planning? . . . Is there a single country whose economic life, over a period of years, has been guided by an economic plan so that the targets set in the plan bear a modest resemblance to events as they actually occur? No doubt each reader will be tempted to furnish the one case he has heard about. The last two suggested to me were Ceylon and Pakistan. Yet the very fact (as anyone can verify by posing the same query) that it is so difficult to think of an example suggests that the record of planning has hardly been brilliant. For all we know the few apparent successes (if there are any) constitute no more then random occurrences. Despite the absence of evidence on behalf of its positive accomplishments, planning has retained its status as a universal nostrum.[14]

And then there is Friedmann, who proposes that the traditional tripartite scheme of analysis, plan, and action be collapsed into a two-part model in which the step of designing the plan disappears altogether, leaving only analysis and action as the two principal components of a single process.

> As my Venezuelan study had shown, the role of the plan was only incidental to effective planning. Coping successfully with the future was the new objective; the patterning of the relevant information flows became central to the art of planning, which was no longer to be separated from action.[15]

The views about comprehensive rational planning in the above examples are somewhat at odds with the assumptions underlying HUD's stress on rational planning and the development of technically sophisticated comprehensive planning documents prior to the action year. Was this requirement, then, entirely without utility? It may have served a latent function of giving some assurance to HUD that the programs funded would operate in an efficient manner consistent with the agency's objectives. While there is, of course, no way to guarantee this, a well-designed plan serves to approximate such an assurance, *at least on paper.* Thus, to the extent that the CDPs were planning documents of good quality, HUD could be satisfied that its responsibilities as a funding agency were being conscientiously discharged. Moreover, the requirements outlined for the CDPs allowed HUD to exercise influence over local priorities.

But regardless of the extent to which the emphasis on an analytically sophisticated approach to planning served HUD's organizational interests, a major question still remains as to whether, in terms of intended consequences, the quality of the plan made a positive difference in what followed during the action year.

The relationships between our measures of CDP quality and the achievement of performance objectives are summarized in table 8-2. The findings here are mixed, with more than half of the correlations either negligible or in the negative direction. Depending upon the specific criteria of CDP quality, we can infer from these data various answers to the question of whether the quality of the plan had any effect upon outcomes. There are some interesting contrasts in the degree to which each criterion of CDP quality is associated with the measures of program outcome.

The deskmen's qualitative ratings of CDPs ("best/worst") show a strong positive association with the measures of program implementation (implementation of coordination, gamma .782 and implementation of citizen participation, gamma .695). This suggests that cities that produced the CDPs that stood out as the "best" plans as judged by federal staff were more likely to have done a better a job of involving agencies and citizens in the implementation process than cities with CDPs that were rated among the "worst." In addition, cities with the "best" CDPs were also more likely to have been judged among the most successful on overall program performance during the action year (gamma .770). However, there is a large discrepancy between these substantial relationships to performance ratings and the ability of these cities to actually deliver services as indicated by the negligible relationships of CDP ratings and spending patterns. Thus, it appears that in terms of the subjective ratings of federal officials of CDP quality the "best" plans may well produce positive results, at least with regard to the achievement of process objectives of implementation. But cities with the best CDPs are not more likely than other cities to create new programs and deliver services within their proposed schedule. This, of course, raises questions about whether there is a link between process objectives and the implementation and delivery of services (which we will shortly examine).

The second criterion of CDP quality is the number of agencies designated in the plan to assume formal responsibilities for carrying out projects. As noted earlier in chapter 6, this measure is used to

Table 8-2. Associations Between Measures of CDP Quality and Other Model Cities Planning Objectives (Gammas)

	Judgments of "Best/Worst" CDPs	Number of Agencies Designated in the CDP	Percent of Categorical Funds in the CDP	Percent of Local Funds in the CDP
Outcome Measures of the Implementation Process				
Implementation of coordination	.782	−.411	.296	.167
Implementation of citizen participation	.695	−.164	.405	−.176
Outcome Measures of Program Performance				
Percent supplemental funds spent six months	−.046	.025	.210	−.067
Percent supplemental funds spent twelve months	.031	.041	.440	−.082
Per capita MNA spending at twelve months	.0	−.046	.422	−.215
Ratings of "most/least" successful programs	.770	−.262	.297	−.019

infer the extent to which the CDPs were responsible to HUD's coordination-of-service requirements. The data in table 8-2 indicate the unanticipated and rather important findings about the relationship between this criterion of CDP quality and the measures of program outcome we discussed in chapter 6. That is, of the three CDP criteria, this measure of quality is more likely to be negatively related to program outcomes than any others. Cities that obtained the largest number of agency commitments in their CDPs produced the weakest record on both implementation objectives and program performance objectives.

The third criterion of CDP quality is the percent of categorical funds in the CDP budget, which, as already noted, is positively associated with the six outcome measures. Among the three criteria of CDP quality, the percent of categorical funds is the only measure that is related to a meaningful degree in a positive direction with *all* the outcome variables of process and program performance. Cities that acquired a high proportion of categorical funds in their CDP budgets tended to excel in the implementation phase of the program. Indeed, if percent of categorical funds was the only criterion of CDP quality, the link between the merit of the planning product and implementation would appear rather firm.

The relationship between the percent of categorical funds in the CDP budget and program performance (as measured by spending patterns during the program year) are of particular significance. The data indicate that cities with CDP budgets that incorporated a high percent of categorical funding were usually more effective than those with low categorical funding in expenditures of supplemental monies on program development and service delivery. This relationship is of interest because it is the strongest link between a measure of the quality of the plan and patterns of expenditure as outcome measures of program performance in the chain of planning objectives.

Why would the acquisition of commitments of categorical funds in the planning phase be strongly associated with the spending of supplemental monies when the program went into operation? On its face, the reasons for this relationship are not obvious. But there are a few plausible lines of explanation. In chapter 3, we noted that the percent of categorical funds in the CDP is used as an indicator of a city's capacity to satisfy HUD's objectives concerning the concentration and mobilization of resources. Assuming that this measure is an accurate indicator, it is quite possible that there is a high degree of transferrability of the skills and capacity of the action system to assemble resources resulting in the ability to move effectively into the next stage; that is, a capacity to reach an articulated agreement

on a coordination plan is related to a capacity for program implementation and the spending of funds on program development.

While this may partially explain the relationship between obtaining categorical funds and spending supplemental monies, there is
another factor to consider that goes a bit deeper than the presence of
able personnel in the action system. When assembling resources and
securing commitments of funds from agencies in the interorganizational field, it is certainly advantageous to possess leverage in the
broader political arena. Many agencies might be willing to negotiate
with the CDA in the anticipation of obtaining supplemental funds to
expand their operations. However, getting them to commit their own
categorical monies to the Model Cities Program is quite another
matter. In approaching agencies on this matter, CDA staff can appeal
to their sense of higher purpose, emphasizing the professional values
attendant on rational planning and community development objectives. Or a case can be made for committing categorical funds to the
Model Cities enterprise on the basis of enlightened self-interest. But
the logic and persuasiveness of these efforts notwithstanding, in the
final analysis the presence of vigorous support from the local chief
executive appears to have a substantial influence on the CDA's capacity to secure categorical funds from local agencies. As reported in
chapter 6, our findings indicate a strong correlation (gamma .534)
between the degree of chief executive support and the percent of
categorical funds in the CDP budget. In addition, we found a substantial degree of association between chief executive support and
the percent of supplemental funds spent at twelve months (gamma
.455) and per capita spending at twelve months (gamma .789). These
data suggest that chief executive support may be the major factor
underlying the relationship between categorical funding and the
spending of supplemental monies. That is, it appears that the same
political pressure from the city chief executive that was exercised to
help secure categorical funds for the CDP was available and used to
push for program implementation when HUD's urgent concerns over
the high rates of underspending in the first six months of the action
year were conveyed to the Model Cities.

The last of the "planning products" is the percent of local funds in
the CDP. It can be noted that there are negative associations between
percent local and five of the six outcome measures. The one
positive association, between percent local and implementation of
coordination, is low (gamma .167). These associations support our
original expectations about this CDP characteristic. That is, those
cities that had higher percentages of local funds in their CDPs were
more likely than others to have both staff-dominant patterns of

influence (gamma –.161) and chief executives with strong commitment to the program (gamma .395). These CDAs were less likely than others to have developed positive working relationships either with agencies or with residents. This is reflected in the generally low-to-negligible negative associations between this variable and program outcomes.

IMPLEMENTATION PROCESS AND PROGRAM PERFORMANCE

The final link in the chain of planning objectives is between two dimensions of program output: the process of implementation and program development. The process of implementation objectives refer to how cities went about putting their plans into action. A "good" process sought to harmonize the program development and service-delivery efforts of participating agencies and to maintain a high degree of accountability to local residents. Program performance objectives refer to how well the cities developed programs in line with the program projections in their CDPs. Did they spend the funds granted, build programs, and produce concrete results within the planned time frame? The quality of the results produced is, of course, the ultimate test of program performance objectives. However, because of the difficulty of obtaining qualitative measures of program output, funding agencies must often settle for surrogate measures such as concrete results showing the numbers of programs in operation, numbers of staff delivering services, numbers of clients served, and the like. This was clearly the case in Model Cities where, as James observes:

> "Delivery of services" was a phrase that acquired significance as the program developed. It represented the desire of program managers to show visible accomplishments, and also served as a substitute goal, excusing their failure to achieve others. The mere fact of having delivered a "service," regardless of its individual merit or relation to other activities, served the dual function of avoiding focus on other problems and providing a sense of practical accomplishment.[16]

As we noted in chapter 6, HUD, like other federal agencies that make grants to local communities, is sensitive about grantees expending federal funds within the fiscal year. While "spending the money" was not phrased as an explicit objective, producing concrete results and delivering services does require the expenditure of substantial proportions of grants. In private conversations with the authors, some of the HUD officials referred to "underspending" as a serious failure in program performance.

As with the other links in HUD's planning model, it is assumed that the implementation process will be compatible with, and instrumental to, the timely production of concrete results. Yet there is potential for conflict between these planning objectives. Efforts to implement the coordination of service delivery involve negotiating and settling new boundaries in the task environment of participating agencies. Although some of this work may have been accomplished in the planning phase, many of the details of coordination activities cannot be settled until the individuals and agencies involved begin to implement coordination according to the agreed upon guidelines. And often what is agreed upon in principle meets resistance when translated into action. Coordinating agency staff need to establish relationships with the staff of the other agencies participating in the program. Arrangements must be agreed upon for supervision, responsibility for scheduling meetings, setting the agendas, professional status alignments, and systems of accountability.[17] And the interorganizational strains that develop as participating agencies strive to balance their involvement in the coordination enterprise with their desire to retain autonomy in their sphere of service delivery must be resolved. In all, operationalizing the new sets of relationships is a time-consuming effort. As noted in the findings from a study of thirty service-coordination projects funded by HEW:

> Service integration is an evolutionary process. It takes time for service integration to occur—time for organization and implementation of a project, time for a project to attain legitimacy in the eyes of service providers, and time for participating agencies to develop a comfortable working relationship, often a necessary prerequisite to the coordination or consolidation of agency functions.[18]

Given that coordination of service delivery is an evolutionary, time-consuming process, it might be reasonably anticipated that a high degree of achievement on this objective would be coupled with a slow record of progress on program development, with the achievement of concrete results awaiting the cementing of interorganizational relationships. This expectation, of course, is contrary to the positive reinforcement of objectives implied in HUD's model. However, as illustrated in table 8-3, neither our own nor HUD's expectation is supported by the findings. That is, rather than a strong positive or a strong negative relationship, the achievement of coordination objectives had a negligible degree of association with program

Table 8-3. Associations Between Outcome Measures of Implementation Process and Program Performance

Program Performance Measures	Implementation of Coordination	Implementation of Citizen Participation
Percent supplemental funds spent 6 months	.138	.104
Percent supplemental funds spent twelve months	.080	.223
Per capita expenditures at twelve months	.222	.356
Ratings of "most/least" successful programs	.783	.513

performance as measured by spending patterns. There was a moderate relationship between the implementation of citizen participation and spending patterns. Although relationships with spending patterns were not strong, the achievement level on both process objectives was highly correlated with the federal officials' ratings of the "most successful" programs (gammas .783 and .513). We should note that these subjective ratings of program success also correlated highly with spending patterns (percent and per capita expenditures at 12 months: gammas .552 and .459).

Thus, it appears that from the federal perspective the achievement of process objectives was viewed as an important outcome measure independent of the extent to which it was directly associated with spending patterns. This can be understood because the pressure to produce concrete results and spend the funds granted within the program year emanated more from the political exigencies of the federal budgeting process than from technical principles of good planning. Since Model Cities was slated to be an ongoing program, HUD officials, although somewhat dismayed by underspending, could take the long-range view and responded favorably to cities that realized process objectives. That is, the view of HUD administrators appears to have been that although program development in these cities was a bit behind schedule in the first year, at least these cities would ultimately build a base of interorganizational relationships and citizen participation that was well integrated and functionally able to implement their programs.

SUMMARY

In this chapter we explored the relationships among the various links in the chain of planning objectives for Model Cities, based upon a series of outcome measures that approximate these objectives. The findings reveal both strong and weak relationships depending upon how the performance criteria for different outcomes were operationally defined. While not entirely unequivocal, the findings lend a reasonable degree of support to the assumption that the links in HUD's chain of planning objectives were connected in a positive manner. These findings and some of the underlying factors that might account for the apparent strengths and weaknesses in HUD's model are summarized below.

Patterns of Influence

The degree of citizen influence in the planning process had a curvilinear relationship to the other program outcomes. Cities that fell into the extreme categories of either staff dominance or citizen dominance were more likely to score low on all other outcome measures of performance than those that fell into the middle-range category of parity in the planning process. On its face, this relationship suggests that, within the bounds of moderation, citizen influence in the planning process is instrumental to the achievement of other objectives. At the same time there are a number of underlying factors associated with the development of parity arrangements that might further account for the relatively high achievements of cities with this pattern of influence. As noted in chapter 4, parity patterns of influence tended to develop in action systems where the sociopolitical environment was comparatively stable and well integrated. These characteristics of the sociopolitical environment in which planning occurred would seem to set parity cities off on a smooth course toward future program developments irrespective of the substantive quality of citizen input into the planning process. Moreover, in our view, to create and sustain the parity arrangement required a high level of professional skill on the part of CDA staff and positive attitudes of trust and cooperation on the part of resident groups. These skills and attitudes are applicable not only to building a planning network but also to the achievement of other program objectives. Thus, while parity cities were "high achievers" on program objectives, attempts to understand the dynamics of this relationship must take into consideration a host of interdependent factors the weightings of which are unknown.

Quality of the CDP

The association between the quality of the CDP and outcomes in the first action year varies in strength and direction depending upon which of the four criteria of CDA quality is considered. On two of the four criteria of CDP quality, relationships to outcomes measures were generally positive, and about half of these positive relationships were in the moderate-to-strong range. Thus, cities that produced CDPs judged technically superior by federal officials were likely to perform well on implementation objectives and to receive high scores on the overall ratings of program success. However, as reflected in spending patterns, these cities did not do appreciably better on the timely delivery of concrete results than cities that produced inferior planning products.

The data also reveal positive relationships between all of the outcome measures and CDPs that achieved relatively high degrees of resource mobilization (operationally defined by the percent of categorical funds in the CDP budget). Among these relationships the most prominent finding was the substantial association between percent of categorical funds in the CDP and spending patterns for twelve months. That cities with high percents of categorical funds had a better record in spending their grants within the stipulated fiscal period may be explained tentatively by the fact that in both cases chief executive support tended to be strong. The implication here is that the chief executive's political support had a catalytic effect on CDA efforts to mobilize resources and to activate the program. This crucial function of local political support is suggested in the report of a case study of ten Model Cities which notes: "CDA ability to obtain agency participation was closely linked to the degree of chief executive support."[19]

The third and fourth criteria of CDP quality, the number of agencies designated in the CDP to play a role in the program and percent of local funds in the CDP budget were used as indicators of both the plan's comprehensiveness and the degree of coordination it was designed to effect, and degree of local governmental support. Of the four criteria, these were the weaker links to the achievement of outcome objectives, with relationships to outcome measures either negligible or in the negative direction. The explanation suggested for these findings is, first, that in cities with large numbers of agencies in their CDPs, there was a certain deficiency in the CDA's skill and judgment with regard to the interpretation of HUD's mandate for comprehensive planning. While HUD guidelines on this objective (pp. 11-12) imply a broad, all-encompassing approach, James suggests that the degree of comprehensiveness actually intended was not necessarily that ambitious.

> The insistence on comprehensive planning was, in part, an effort to increase the emphasis on social planning, so that social programs and services would be instituted early in the Model Cities program, giving direct tangi-

ble benefits well before the period required by completion of a physical project. Therefore, it was probably more a demand for balanced planning than for a high degree of rationality and coverage.[20]

Given the ambiguity of what HUD meant by comprehensiveness, it would appear that planners who went all out to involve relatively large numbers of agencies probably lacked sophistication and over-extended their reach in their efforts to interpret the degree of comprehensiveness necessary to satisfy HUD requirements. In this case, then, the poor record of performance on outcome objectives is related to the implied lack of planning skills and compounded by the complications of trying to implement a new program designed with too many parts.

The poor performance of cities that achieved higher percentages of local funds in their CDP budget is not, of course, attributable to the local funds themselves. Rather, the higher percent of local funds is a reflection that these cities tended to be staff dominant and were less effective than other cities at involving both agencies and residents in planning.

Program Outcomes

In examining program outcomes we focused on the relationships between process and performance objectives. The findings show that achievement on process objectives had weak-to-negligible associations with performance (measured in terms of expenditure patterns within the grant period from which we infer service-delivery output). This probably reflects some of the inherent strains between political pressures to produce swift tangible results for congressional and public recognition, and professional ambitions for efficient implementation of the program according to carefully designed administrative processes. Yet the strain was not so great as to result in clearly negative relationships between these objectives. Despite the weak relationships between process objectives and expenditure patterns, federal ratings of program success were strongly correlated with the achievement of process objectives. At the same time, these success ratings were also closely associated with the cities' ability to spend the action-year grant monies. Thus, from the federal perspective, at least for the first action year, process measures of outcome were as important in judging program success as the achievement of concrete results reflected in expenditure patterns. Apparently, HUD's desire to satisfy political needs for visible results was balanced by its staunch commitment to orderly and rational program development which was part of the chain of objectives.

NOTES

1. See John Friedmann, *Retracking America: A Theory of Transactive Planning* (New York: Doubleday, 1973).

2. Neil Gilbert and Joseph Eaton, "Who Speaks for the Poor?", *Journal of the American Institute of Planners* 36, no. 6 (November 1970): 412.

3. Warner Bloomberg, Jr. and Florence W. Rosenstock, "Who Can Activate the Poor—One Assessment of Maximum Feasible Participation," in *Poverty and Urban Policy*, eds. Warner Bloomberg and Henry J. Schmandt (Beverly Hills: Sage Publications, Inc., 1968).

4. U.S. Department of Housing and Urban Development, *Citizen Organizations: Model Cities Management Series, Bulletin No. 6* (Washington, D.C.: Government Printing Office, 1971), p. 3.

5. Gilbert and Eaton.

6. Charles F. Grosser, "Middle Class Professionals—Lower Class Clients" (New York: Columbia University, Unpublished Dissertation, 1963).

7. Ronald Lippitt, et al., *The Dynamics of Planned Change* (New York: Harcourt, Brace, and World, Inc., 1958), p. 66.

8. Samuel P. Huntington, "The Democratic Distemper," *The Public Interest* 41 (Fall 1975): 9-35.

9. See, for example, Charles E. Lindblom, "The Science of 'Muddling Through,' " *Public Administration Review* 19 (Spring 1959): 79-88.

10. Peter Rossi and Robert Dentler, *The Politics of Urban Renewal* (New York: The Free Press, 1969), p. 286.

11. It should be noted that by 1971 the question of HUD's intentions regarding the degree of citizen participation was settled in favor of parity arrangements, as stated in HUD, *Citizen Organizations*, p. 3: "Clearly HUD had in mind a partnership and cooperative agreement between the city and the community, although it refrained from determining the 'ideal' organizational structure and relationships." The wording here suggests a greater clarity and consensus of intention than existed among HUD officials in 1967.

12. While Model Cities planning was extensive in comparison to that of the antipoverty program, a critical assessment suggests that the one-year planning period was unrealistically short in light of HUD's rigorous requirements. This is borne out by the fact that many CDP submissions ran well over the twelve-month deadline.

13. Francine Rabinovitz, *City Politics and Planning* (New York: Atherton, 1969), pp. 6-7.

14. Aaron Wildavsky, "Does Planning Work?" *The Public Interest* 24 (Summer 1971); 95-96.

15. Friedmann, pp. 16-17.

16. Judson Lehman James, "Federalism and the Model Cities Experiment," paper delivered at the Annual Meeting of the American Political Science Association, Los Angeles, September 1970, p. 7.

17. For a case analysis of some of the problems that arose as these questions were addressed in a coordination project in the antipoverty program, see Neil

Gilbert, "Neighborhood Coordinator: Advocate or Middleman?" *Social Service Review* 43, no. 2 (June 1969): 136-44.

18. U.S. Department of Health, Education, and Welfare, *Integration of Human Services in HEW: An Evaluation of Service Integration Projects*, vol. 1 (Washington, D.C.: Government Printing Office, 1972), p. 16.

19. U.S. Department of Housing and Urban Development, *The Model Cities Program: Ten Model Cities—A Comparative Analysis of Second Round Planning Year* (Washington, D.C.: Government Printing Office, 1974), p. 63.

20. James, p. 9.

❋ Chapter 9

Planning to Plan: An Assessment of Predictions About Model Cities Participants

Prior to implementation of the Model Cities Program, federal planners designed and participated in a set of procedures to select program participants. This rather substantial effort was aimed at rating all cities that applied for initial planning grants according to their capacities to realize the program's objectives. This chapter analyzes those selection procedures and the ability of Model Cities planners to predict the applicants' performance on major program objectives.

PICKING WINNERS: THE BASES FOR PLANNING GRANT ALLOCATIONS

Picking winners is an objective of all administrators and planners who have the difficult task of allocating resources within and among large bureaucratic agencies. The perennial question of how to select from among organizations, agencies, and cities that apply for funds (usually federal) is frequently settled on political grounds or on the basis of the granting officer's personal knowledge of the applicants. However, when the number of applicants is larger than the number to be selected, and when the granting authority is composed of many actors, political considerations and the knowledge that comes from direct personal experience may not be sufficient. The granting authority may then attempt to utilize objective and technical means for assessing the merits of the different applicants. A good deal of evaluative research is directed at the development of instruments that can measure such obscure characteristics as the abilities, weaknesses, and success potential of applicants. Before examining the instruments and procedures used by the Department of Housing and Urban Development (HUD) to select the first seventy-five cities that received planning grants for Model Cities, a few comments on the general trend in grant allocation methods are in order.

The Burden of Discretion in Fund Allocation

The most significant feature of revenue sharing is that federal discretion is reduced in the allocation of funds to local areas.[1] Under revenue-sharing arrangements, judgments of federal staff as a major input in selection of the localities eligible for funds have seen severely curtailed. How much shared revenue local communities receive and what they can spend it for is, by and large, determined by formula. At present, neither the general, nor most of the special, revenue-sharing programs have developed performance criteria with which localities must comply to become eligible for funds or for refunding.[a]

The intention of the federal administration under the "New Federalism" is to displace the categorical grant-in-aid system of federal financing with revenue-sharing programs.[2] Under the grant-in-aid system, the judgments of federal staff were of great importance in determining who was to receive funds and the purposes for which funds might be used. Even in the use of supplemental funds in the Model Cities Program, which were in effect "bloc grants" providing some of the flexibility of revenue sharing, the selection of the cities to participate in the program involved a high degree of federal discretion. Among other criteria, applicants were judged on their potential capacity to carry out program objectives.[3]

While federal discretion in fund allocation is considerably diminished under revenue sharing, it is not entirely eliminated. As revenue-sharing programs develop, it can be expected that federal goals will gradually come to be reflected in performance criteria for state and local jurisdictions receiving federal funds. Ultimately, receipt of all federal revenue-sharing funds may require prior approval of local plans. The latter requirement is made clear in the authorization of the Law Enforcement Assistance Administration through 1976 (P.L. 93-138) and the Older Americans Service Amendments of 1973 (P.L. 93-29).[4]

Of course, the current deemphasis of federal discretion and control places greater responsibility and authority on the states and

---

[a]Some special revenue sharing programs such as Title XX of the 1974 Amendments to the Social Security Act (P.L. 93-647) and the Housing and Community Development Act of 1974 (P.L. 93-383) do include specific performance criteria.

other large jurisdictions to exercise discretion and control. While the shift from federal control to state and local control reduces the scope of bureaucratic discretion involved in allocations, the requirement for such discretion is by no means eliminated. In 1967, twenty-four states had over 1000 units of local government, with Illinois topping the list at 6500 units.[5] Therefore, whether handled by the federal government or the states, the problems related to allocations and the need for technical ability to judge and select among large numbers of applicants for funds will continue to be relevant for community planning. The Model Cities experience provides an opportunity to explore the rationale for such selection procedures and how these procedures may be organized and conducted.

Design of the Planning Grant Review Project

HUD's selection process for choosing the cities to receive Model Cities planning grants incorporated a high degree of federal discretion. The assumption was that by using expert judgments made by federal staff they could pick winners; that is, they could select those applicants most likely to achieve Model Cities Program objectives better than could be done by random choice, or by a first-come, first-served method, or by some other system of selection. By comparing the federal ratings given to applicants with measures of actual program outcomes, we attempt to determine the extent to which this assumption provides a useful guide for grant-allocation policy.

The first major task confronting the Model Cities Administration (MCA) in launching the program was to select the cities to receive planning grants. All cities were eligible to submit applications for grants. By May 1, 1967, the deadline for submissions, 193 cities had applied. Six months later, on November 16, 1967, the first sixty-three cities to receive grants were announced, and twelve more were named during the spring of 1968. In all, seventy-five cities were selected from the original 193 applicants for first-round-funding. The cities and towns chosen had populations ranging in size from approximately 2300 to 8,000,000.

The preparation of the application for a planning grant was no simple matter. In effect, the cities were asked to submit a "plan to plan." Willmann notes that Philadelphia, which submitted a 350-page proposal for a planning grant, was "an outstanding example of the kind of planning necessary for model city activity."[6] From HUD's perspective, putting the application together was an initial test of the city's potential for meeting the more extensive planning requirements and program objectives that would be expected of cities participating in the program. It was from this perspective that an intricate and costly project was established to review and compare applications for the purpose of awarding the first-round Model Cities planning grants.

The procedure for choosing among applicants was called the Planning Grant Review Project (PGRP). The PGRP was a systematic attempt to analyze and evaluate all of the applicant cities and the applications they submitted. Initially, applications were reviewed, commented upon, and rated by members of each of the agencies expected to be engaged in funding demonstrations projects: HUD, Department of Justice, Department of Health, Education and Welfare (HEW), Office of Economic Opportunity (OEO), and the Departments of Labor, Transportation, and Commerce. Following this review, there was a preliminary interagency review committee meeting in which decisions were made either to defer the application or to move it to an "advanced review" at which point the final funding recommendation was made. Based upon the final recommendations at the advanced review, HUD made the selection of cities to be funded, subject to White House approval.

Of course, the final selection of cities was not a purely technical matter based on expert judgments of capability. Political considerations also played a role in this process. At the very least, a wide geographical spread among the chosen cities was politically desirable. And there is reason to believe that in some cases more stringent political constraints were operating. For example, it is not surprising that in a Congress dominated by Democrats, only nine of the first sixty-three cities chosen were represented in the House of Representatives by Republicans. Five of the cities chosen were in districts of administration supporters on the House HUD-Independent Offices Appropriations Subcommittee.[7] One of these cities, Smithville, Tennessee (population approximately 2300), was represented by the subcommittee's chairman. Later, Smithville received a substantial action grant for the first program year. Asked to explain Smithville's good fortune, former HUD Undersecretary Wood said: "Smithville is a very small place, but there are those who love it."[8] Similarly, James notes that although Alberquerque, New Mexico officials spent only six days preparing their application, they were confident that Senator Clinton Anderson would not be refused, and they were right.[9] On the other hand, Charlotte, North Carolina was selected despite the fact that its congressman was one of the most vigorous House opponents of Model Cities. This suggests that, as with many federal allocations, the Planning Grant Review Project (PGRP) may be seen as an effort to exercise discretion and technical expertise *within the broad political boundaries of choice.* This interpretation allows the possibility that the PGRP was an elaborate device to rationalize the degree of discretion available to program planners within the boundaries of predetermined political choice. If this was the case, it was not a very useful effort from the viewpoint of efficiency. As we shall note, a tremendous amount of time and money went into this selection procedure.

In the PGRP there were two main dimensions along which applicants were evaluated by each federal agency. These dimensions were conceived of as a *capability analysis* and a *functional analysis.* The *capability analysis* was primarily an evaluation of the applicant's general capacity for meeting the Model Cities Program objectives as judged by experience and performance in related programs. For example, a typical HEW capability report is summarized thus:

> [The applicant] rated above-average in ability to develop, execute, and support a coordinated MNA program. Communications across organizational lines, with client groups and individual citizens has been effective and maintained. County schools enjoy excellent leadership and history of cooperative enterprise. There has been a "creative" response to a potentially overwhelming Cuban refugee problem. Schools, public welfare and state Vocational Rehabilitation all rated better than average.[10]

HUD's capability reports were the most systematic. They were usually based on input obtained from HUD regional staff, who rated the city's experience and performance in the areas of urban renewal, public housing, relocation, workable program, and equal opportunity.

The *functional analysis* focused upon the substance of the application. Reviewers sought to evaluate the quality and coherence of the problem analysis, program approaches, and objectives. For example, the following comments are reported in the staff summary of an advanced review:

> Though he says goals and objectives are clearly stated, Washington reader is left with impression that the city feels there is little wrong with its past performance and that the trouble lies with the people who need changing more than the structures in which they live (a comment bearing more on problem analysis than on goals, priorities, program strategy, and approach). Regional reviewer sees lack of concreteness in problem analysis reflected in goals and program approaches; cites absence of priorities and program strategy.[11]

In addition, the proposed planning structure was carefully reviewed with an eye on the applicant's translation of the citizen participation requirement into operational procedures. Some cities rated high on this criterion as exemplified by one review statement that "the applicant presents a thoughtful and innovative proposal designed to place power to plan and implement the program in the hands of neighborhood residents."[12] Other cities appeared to miss the mark:

> [The applicant] proposes a minimal citizen participation mechanism which can only be characterized as tight-fisted. Not only does the Mayor have total control over who shall be appointed to the citizen participation panel, but the panel itself does not participate in policy making as prescribed by the law and is limited to "discussing and reacting" to ideas presented to it by the city. Additionally, the average resident is barred from being considered for appointment because the majority of citizens' seats will go to property owners.[13]

Of the various agencies involved in the PGRP, HEW conducted the most systematic functional review of applications by means of a rating scale on which reviewers gave cities numerical scores. The HEW analysis of applications was divided into five areas: objectives, methods of reaching goals, innovative approaches, administrative machinery, and problem analysis. Each of these areas was rated on a five-point scale, and the area ratings were weighted differentially according to HEW's estimates of their importance. The average score given to cities was 60 out of a possible 100 points.

As this description suggests, the PGRP was a costly and time-consuming operation. It required that high-level officials of various federal agencies read numerous applications, comment on them in writing, and discuss them in committee meetings. HUD had to make some decisions based upon the information, opinions, and data gathered. The knowledge, experience, and expert judgments of the professional staff of many different agencies was utilized in a concerted effort to exercise federal discretion fairly, systematically, and intelligently. The objective of all this activity was to select from among 193 applicants the seventy-five cities that appeared most capable of carrying out the planning process envisioned by HUD and implementing plans after they were approved. Recognizing that, without the PGRP, about twenty-nine of the seventy-five cities finally selected through the PGRP would probably have been chosen anyhow by simple random selection, it is useful to ask whether this monumental effort made any difference. In an attempt to shed some light on this question we compare the federal ratings given applicants in the PGRP with measures of performance. These performance measures are concerned with the planning process, the product, and implementation.

Planning Grant Review Project Ratings

To estimate the extent to which federal judgments made during the selection process were predictive of program outcomes, we compared the ratings given to the cities' applications in the Planning Grant Review Project (PGRP) with the cities' performances on each of five program outcome indicators. The PGRP ratings were taken from the review committee summaries on each city. With the exception of the HEW numerical functional ratings, these ratings were in the form of qualitative statements on selection criteria. To transform these qualitative data to quantitative ratings in order to make statistical comparisons, the documents on each city were independently reviewed by three coders with instructions to rank the city from poor to excellent based upon the PGRP qualitative judgments on the following four selection criteria:

1. *Overall Capability*, a rating of the city's potential for planning and implementation according to HUD guidelines based on prior experience in related programs;
2. *HEW Functional Rating*, the numerical rating that HEW staff gave each city according to the formula they developed for analyzing applications;
3. *Citizen Participation*, a rating of how well the city was expected to implement citizen participation in the planning process based on the structure described in their application; and
4. *Technical Quality*, an overall rating of the technical quality of the city's application.

Three coders each independently reviewed the review committee summaries on all seventy-five cities. Where two of the three coders agreed, the ranking on a variable was accepted; otherwise the city was given no score for that variable. The data in table 9-1 indicate that there were moderate-to-high correlations among the selection criteria ratings. The rating of technical quality is the single variable most strongly associated with the other ratings. These relationships suggest that there was a fair degree of internal consistency among the PGRP ratings. But the correlations are not so high as to require treating the selection criteria ratings as equivalent measures.

Before we move on to a description of the findings, one major caveat is in order. Interpretation of the findings is limited in a significant way because our comparative analysis deals only with those cities finally selected to participate. We have not included PGRP ratings for the rejected cities because, of course, we have no evidence

Table 9-1. Associations Among PGRP Selection Criteria Ratings (Gammas)

	Overall Capability	Technical Quality	Citizen Participation
Technical Quality	.660	—	—
Citizen Participation	.530	.672	—
HEW Functional Rating	.440	.666	.397

about how the rejected cities might have fared in respect to the performance criteria. More than half of the cities that applied for first-round funding were rejected, presumably in most cases because they received lower ratings in the PGRP than those cities selected. Thus, what this analysis focuses upon is the PGRP's ability to estimate the relative potential for performance among those cities ostensibly considered the best of the applicants; it makes comparisons among those not rejected. In this sense it may be that our data reveal how well the PGRP could rank those cities within the "winner's circle," assuming a degree of accuracy in the initial rejections. If this is the case, then even a moderate degree of success should be considered quite impressive.

SELECTION CRITERIA AND PROGRAM PERFORMANCE

We have selected five indicators of performance for comparison with the Planning Grant Review Project (PGRP) ratings:

1. degree of citizen influence in the planning process;
2. overall quality of the Comprehensive Demonstration Plan (CDP);
3. percent of CDP budget composed of categorical funds;
4. first program-year expenditures for service delivery (percent of supplemental funds spent in the first twelve months of the program year); and
5. per capita first program-year expenditures for social service delivery (per capita supplemental funds spent per MNA resident in the first twelve months of the program year).

To what extent did the four PGRP ratings of cities' potential for program implementation correspond with the actual performance of the cities in terms of the five performance criteria? An approximate answer to this question may be found by examining the relationships between the PGRP ratings and ratings on performance criteria shown in table 9-2. The general pattern of findings indicates that the results were mixed, but on the whole were not very encouraging with regard

Table 9-2. Associations Between Planning Grant Review Project and Performance Indicators (Gammas)

Performance Indicators	PGRP Ratings			
	Overall Capability	*HEW Functional Rating*	*Citizen Participation*	*Technical Quality*
Citizen Influence in the Planning Process	.377	.290	.454	.154
Overall Quality of the CDP	.091	.211	.305	.178
Percent of CDP Budget Composed of Categorical Funds	−.453	−.332	−.121	−.222
First Program-Year Expenditures	−.321	.173	.002	.036
Per Capita First Program-Year Expenditures	.035	−.102	.154	.103

to the accuracy of PGRP ratings of the applicants' potential for satisfying the various objectives of the Model Cities Program. In 30 percent of the cells, correlations are in the negative direction, in which cases the high PGRP ratings of potential are associated with low performance ratings. Thus, for example, cities rated high on overall capability based on the PGRP staff assessments of their prior experience actually tended to perform worse with regard to the acquisition of categorical funds (gamma −.453) and to spending in terms of the percent of supplemental funds (gamma −.321) than cities that were judged to have low capability. Only 25 percent of the cells show moderate positive correlations between PGRP ratings and performance, with the remaining cells showing positive correlations that are low or negligible (gammas less than .200).

The sharpest distinction that emerges from these findings is that the PGRP ratings are most strongly and consistently associated in a positive direction with performance ratings of citizen influence in the planning process. Indeed, the strongest positive correlation in table 9-2 is between the PGRP ratings of potential for citizen participation and the performance ratings of citizen influence (gamma .454). And the second rongest correlation is between PGRP ratings of overall capability and performance ratings of citizen influence (gamma .377).

These findings suggest that the PGRP gave special emphasis to assessments of the applicants' plans for citizen participation and the applicants' capacity for implementing this particular objective. The findings apparently reflect the staunch commitment to citizen participation objectives of the HUD administrative staff responsible for the Model Cities Program during this period. This emphasis on citizen participation is confirmed by evidence from other sources which indicates that first-round planning grant awards were often accompanied by stipulations that the city spell out or strengthen its provisions for resident participation in Model Cities planning.[14]

A SIMPLIFIED ALTERNATIVE

The first-round Model Cities could have been selected by a variety of methods utilizing assumptions similar to those on which the PGRP ratings were based. We will conclude this part of the analysis by presenting one example of a simple and inexpensive alternative method for the quantitative rating of applicants and the results obtained when ratings generated by this simplified approach are compared with performance ratings. Our major purpose in presenting this alternative is to illustrate the possibilities of simplified measures and at the same time to provide a comparative set of measures against which the relative utility of the PGRP ratings can be assessed. We do not offer it as a substitute for a PGRP type of selection method or even as a necessarily desirable approach to the selection problem.

In the PGRP, overall capability ratings were based on qualitative judgments of the applicants' past experiences in related program areas. The assumption was that past program experience, including the knowledge, skill, commitment, agency linkages, and other characteristics, would be relevant to an assessment of a city's potential to implement successfully the Model Cities Program.[15] And it was believed that the differential quality of these experiences could be assessed accurately enough to be a useful tool in the selection process. Another approach is simply to assume that *length* of experience in related program areas (for instance, urban renewal) will reflect the development of knowledge, skills, and other characteristics prerequisite for the Model Cities Program. Length of experience might also be used to indicate the speed with which cities respond to opportunities for urban development; the longer a city has been operating a related program, the earlier it submitted an acceptable application for that program and the more time it has had to learn from, and to integrate, its experiences.[16] Based on this assumption, estimates of capability can be derived by calculating the number of years prior to 1967 that applicants had been operating programs in related areas.

For the purposes of this illustration, public housing and urban renewal were selected as related program areas. (Both programs received emphasis in HUD capability ratings in the PGRP.) The applicants' ranks on length of experience in these programs were correlated with performance ratings, the results of which are shown in table 9-3.

Table 9-3. Associations Between Length of Experience and Performance Indicators (Gammas)

	Years of Experience in Urban Renewal and Public Housing	
Performance Indicators	*Number of Years Between First Approval for Urban Renewal Program and 1967[a]*	*Number of Years Between Initial Occupancy of Public Housing and 1967[b]*
Citizen Influence in the Planning Process	.563	.231
Overall Quality of the CDP	.117	.060
Percent of CDP Budget Composed of Categorical Funds	−.288	−.141
First Program-Year Expenditures	−.372	−.099
Per Capita First Program-Year Expenditures	−.227	−.010

[a]Source: *Urban Renewal Directory*, 31 December 1967, Department of Housing and Urban Development.

[b]Source: *Consolidated Development Directory*, Report S-11A, 30 June 1967, Department of Housing and Urban Development.

The data in table 9-3 show that of the ten relationships between performance indicators and applicants' length of experience in the two programs, only four are in the expected positive direction. Similar to the findings in table 9-2 the strongest positive correlations are with citizen influence (gammas .563 and .231), and the other positive correlations are with CDP ratings (gammas .117 and .060). If we compare the length of experience in urban renewal (table 9-3) with the overall capability rating (table 9-2), both of which are based on the same assumption, little difference is found in either the direction or the strength of associations with performance indicators. The largest difference obtained is in regard to citizen influence, where the length of experience (gamma .563) has a *stronger* relationship than the overall capability ratings (gamma .377). In fact, for citizen influence, the performance variable with which the PGRP as a whole was best correlated, none of the PGRP ratings has a stronger correlation than the length of experience in urban renewal. This suggests that if applicants were selected mainly on the basis of their potential for developing active citizen participation in the planning process, length of experience in urban renewal as a selection criterion would have produced as good, if not better, results than the array of qualitative judgments actually employed. As noted in chapter 7, the use of this indicator is not to imply that urban renewal programs were distinguished for the amount of citizen participation they encouraged. Rather, it is the general community organizing experience accumulated by cities engaged in urban renewal programs that provides the skills and linkages for developing active citizen participation.[17]

MANIFEST AND LATENT FUNCTIONS OF SELECTION PROCEDURES

Before attempting to derive some general meaning from these results, let us summarize a number of related points that have been made in this discussion.

In terms of the process:

1. The PGRP was an elaborate and costly exercise in federal discretion that involved various personnel of different departments.
2. Though it was an elaborate process, the PGRP was not very precise in the sense that it lacked an explicit systematic procedure for weighting the variety of qualitative inputs and setting priorities among different objectives.
3. In addition, the PGRP selection process was not an exercise in discretion based on purely rational or technical judgments of capability. Some number of applicants apparently were selected on the basis of political favor, the quality of their submissions notwithstanding.

In terms of outcome:

1. The ratio of applicants to program slots available was such that more than one-third of the applicants selected through the PGRP probably would have been chosen by simple random selection.
2. When the various capability ratings of the cities selected to participate in the program are compared with measures of performance, evidence to support the PGRP ratings in terms of their ability to differentiate potential levels of performance is generally weak, except with regard to citizen participation.
3. The employment of inexpensive and simply constructed measures of the cities' prior experience would have produced estimates of performance generally equivalent to those that emerged from the array of qualitative judgments employed in the PGRP decisions.

Given the constraints, the probabilities of random selection, the somewhat imprecise quality of PGRP measures and decisions, the lack of congruence between PGRP ratings and certain types of performance, and the availability of alternative means for "rational" selection, there is little to justify the PGRP in terms of its manifest function. That is, the time and money spent on this type of selection process do not seem warranted in light of the program outcomes. The PGRP was not especially accurate in "picking winners" with regard to the various HUD objectives. For the one objective, citizen participation, with which PGRP ratings correlate most strongly, a simple and inexpensive alternative rating procedure (length of experience) produced similar results. It is possible, as suggested earlier, that the PGRP was developed as a means of cloaking what were essentially political choices in the guise of technical rationality. If this were the major underlying function, it would certainly be difficult to justify all the energy and expense incurred. More creative and less expensive procedures might have been developed. At the very least, fewer agencies could have been involved.

Was the PGRP merely an example of "bureaucratic aggrandizement" whereby federal staff creates a process that exaggerates the power and importance of their judgments and decisions? The evidence tempts the observer to make such an interpretation. Perhaps to some degree the process rewarded those involved with an inflated sense of importance. But the significance of this self-serving function should not be overestimated. The federal staff in the PGRP generally were in the business of making judgments and allocating funds. In this sense the PGRP did not represent a special opportunity to which they responded with excessive zeal.

There is another interpretation of the latent function served by the PGRP that applies directly to program needs, rather than to the needs of politicians or personal aspirations of federal staff. That is, the primary function of this elaborate process may be seen not as a mechanism for selection, but as a strategy to lay the groundwork for program coordination at the federal level. From this perspective the PGRP provided HUD with an opportunity to engage the support of other federal agencies in the Model Cities enterprise. Whether intended or not, the review of applications and various interagency staff meetings served as a socialization process for the different actors that would be called upon to participate once the program began operations. The involvement of these other agencies at this early stage was a means not only of gathering judgments on selection but was also a means for developing common frames of reference and obtaining commitments to the program.

This latent function of the PGRP seems to have been of particular importance in the Model Cities Program because, as Frieden and

Kaplan note in their account of the historical development of Model Cities:

> None of the members [of the U.S. President's Task Force on Urban Problems, which planned the Model Cities Program] represented the federal bureaucracy itself or had much personal experience with its internal administration ... It worked in great secrecy, and it deliberately avoided contact with federal agencies in its field of concern ... [The *modus operandi* of the Task Force] prevented extensive consultations with Congressional leaders and executive departments which would normally have contributed to the formulation of a program of this importance.[18]

It may be assumed that coordination among federal agencies is difficult to attain under any circumstances. But it is more likely to occur in a program in which the relevant agencies of government play a major role at the start by participating in the meaty and difficult tasks of formulating policy, than in a program that delays their participation to the implementation stage. If this is the case, it follows that the imprecise nature of the PGRP was also functional, inasmuch as it allowed each participating agency to imagine that they exercised more influence than was probably the case. Assessed on the basis of this latent function, the utility and efficiency of selection processes like the PGRP may be more substantial than they appear when such processes are judged only according to their stated purpose. At the very least, in developing programs that require the support and cooperation of a variety of agencies, planners and administrators would do well to contemplate the latent function of a multijudgmental selection process even if, as demonstrated with the PGRP, these processes seem inefficient and inadequate for performing the stated purpose of picking winners.

NOTES

1. *State and Local Fiscal Assistance Act of 1972* (General Revenue Sharing); and four Social and Rehabilitation Service measures. Also, see note 1 to Introduction.

2. *New York Times*, "Excerpts from President Nixon's Budget Message as Presented to Congress," 30 January, 1973.

3. For a more detailed discussion of the relationship between the Model Cities Program and revenue-sharing arrangements, see Marshall Kaplan, "Model Cities and National Urban Policy: The Relevance of Model Cities to General and Special Revenue Sharing," *Planning 1971* (Chicago: American Society of Planning Officials, 1971).

4. See Melvin Mogulof, *Special Revenue Sharing in Support of the Public*

Social Services (Washington, D.C.: The Urban Institute, March 1971), Working Paper: 963-16.

5. U.S. Bureau of the Census, *Statistical Abstracts of the United States, 1971* (Washington, D.C.: Government Printing Office, 1971), p. 397.

6. John B. Willmann, *The Department of Housing and Urban Development* (New York: Praeger Publishers, 1967), p. 113.

7. "CQ Fact Sheet on Model City Grants," *Congressional Quarterly Weekly Report* 25: 2455-58, 1 December, 1967.

8. *New York Times*, 13 July, 1969.

9. Judson L. James, "Federalism and the Model Cities Experiment," Paper delivered at the 1970 Annual Meeting of the American Political Science Association, Los Angeles, September 8-12, 1970, p. 17 (mimeographed).

10. U.S. Department of Housing and Urban Development, Model Cities Administration, *Interagency Review Summary*, 12 May, 1967.

11. U.S. Department of Housing and Urban Development, Model Cities Administration, *Staff Summary*—Advanced Review, 1 June, 1967.

12. U.S. Department of Housing and Urban Development, Model Cities Administration, *Staff Summary*—Advanced Review, n.d.

13. U.S. Department of Housing and Urban Development, Model Cities Administration, *Staff Summary*—Advanced Review, 1 June, 1967.

14. See, for example, Roland Warren, "Model Cities First Round: Politics, Planning, and Participation," *Journal of the American Institute of Planners* 35 (July 1969): 245-52; Department of Housing and Urban Development, *The Model Cities Program: A Comparative Analysis of the Planning Process in Eleven Cities* (Washington, D.C.: Government Printing Office, 1970) and James.

15. This assumption recognizes that over the last decade cities have used, for example, urban renewal programs not only to secure federal funds for themselves, but also to create, outside the city's regular departmental structure, a cadre of professional talent that could be employed in various capacities. "The best local renewal authorities," Wilson observes, "became generalized sources of innovation and policy staffing and their directors became in effect deputy Mayors (and sometimes more than that)." James Q. Wilson, "The Mayors vs. the Cities," *The Public Interest*, 23:3 (Summer 1969), p. 30.

16. The length of time that a city has operated urban renewal and public housing programs has been used in other studies as an indicator of the "speed of community innovation." See Michale Aiken and Robert Alford, "Community Structure and Innovation: The Case of Public Housing," *American Political Science Review*, 64, no. 3 (September 1970): 843-64; and Michael Aiken and Robert Alford, "Community Structure and Innovation: The Case of Urban Renewal," *American Sociological Review*, 35, no. 4 (August 1970): 650-65.

17. For an analysis of how skills and linkages that arise out of prior experience in related programs may be employed for developing structures for community participation, see Neil Gilbert, *Clients or Constituents* (San Francisco: Jossey-Bass, Publishers, 1970), pp. 42-68.

18. Bernard J. Frieden and Marshall Kaplan, *The Politics of Neglect: Urban Aid from Model Cities to Revenue Sharing* (Cambridge, Mass.: MIT Press, 1975), pp. 37, 50.

※ Chapter 10

Applications: Some Guidelines for Community Planning

Our intention in this study has been to analyze how the Model Cities went about the business of program development. By comparing the relative amounts of success the cities had in these efforts we sought to identify some of the significant characteristics that affect community planning, and the relationships among these characteristics. In this concluding section we want to push the study findings a bit further to ask: What can be said of them that is of practical use to the community planning enterprise? The conversion of findings on theoretical relationships among a series of abstract variables into practical advice is a hazardous exercise for both donors and recipients of such advice. The study could not include all the variables that might significantly affect community planning; many of the variables included were based on circumscribed operational measures that simplified the complex phenomena under investigation. Thus, the practical suggestions that follow ought to be considered tentative guidelines that practitioners should use cautiously.

QUANTITATIVE CONSIDERATIONS IN PLANNING

Among the quantitative variables, certain guidelines for planning can be drawn from findings on city size and amount of planning experience, numbers of agencies engaged in program planning and implementation, and the amount of categorical funds contributed by participating agencies.

175

City Size and Amount of Planning Experience

Coordination efforts tend to be most successful in cities of medium size that have at least a moderate amount of planning experience; size and experience are also directly associated with the degree of citizen influence that developed in the planning process. These findings have practical implications for planning policy initiated at the national level.

Specifically, the findings suggest that federal designs for community planning programs should be attentive to the heterogeneous aspects of local communities. Rather than a unitary set of policies applied across the board, such designs might incorporate policy sets that differentiate program requirements, expectations, and resource allocations on the basis of the size and experience of the target communities. For example, communities with little experience in planning social programs are relatively disadvantaged in competing for categorical funds, particularly in programs like Model Cities, which require a high degree of integration of political, organizational, and technical skills. At the federal level, funding agencies such as the Model Cities Administration should take this into account when providing planning supports and assessing community performance.

Number of Participating Agencies

The finding that the number of participating agencies is negatively associated with the success of coordination and other program outcomes draws attention to a practical issue that deserves more consideration. There are physical costs and communications costs associated with bringing together representatives of a large number of agencies in planning and program coordination at the community level, at some point these costs impede effective action.

Community planning agencies are frequently under pressure to involve large numbers of agencies in coordination projects. These pressures usually emanate from funding agencies; sometimes, the professionals in the planning agency may, themselves, believe that "more is better." However, whatever the source of pressure to involve large numbers, planners should resist the "more is better" mentality and should weigh the costs of increasing the quantity of agency involvements.

As for the costs of increasing agency involvement, findings from Model Cities suggests that voluntary organizations were less likely than public agencies to participate in community planning and program implementation. And when private/voluntary agencies did participate, they were more likely than public agencies to withdraw after an initial involvement in planning. Planners, therefore, should court the prospective voluntary organization participant with some degree of caution and should be prepared to invest the amount of time and energy required for adjustments in the existing domain consensus when some private organizations not traditionally associated with social welfare are engaged in community planning efforts. Furthermore, a sensitive appraisal of the private organization's willingness and capacity to deal with new constituencies, along with, perhaps, some anticipatory training in this matter to let the agencies know what they can expect in terms of new constituent pressures, would serve the interests of both planning bodies and potential private agency participants.

Amount of Categorical Funds Contributed by Participating Agencies

The data indicate that cities with CDP budgets that incorporated a high percent of categorical funds were more likely to achieve high ratings on program implementation than cities with low percentages of categorical funding. The implication for planners is that they should concentrate effort primarily upon agencies where there appears to be some readiness not only to take, but also to commit resources to community planning projects. In arranging for this exchange of resources, the planner's objective is to create a degree of organizational interdependence that will cement working relationships among participating agencies. With such a network of relationships firmly established, planning agencies will encounter fewer obstacles to implementation.

QUALITATIVE CONSIDERATIONS IN PLANNING

The findings on qualitative factors that influenced community planning in Model Cities are varied and complex. While it is difficult to sort out all of the relationships among the qualitative factors studied and their practical implications, three—citizen participation, chief executive commitment, and planner roles—stand out as having particularly salient consequences for community planning.

Citizen Participation

The evidence from this study suggests that planning and implementation of programs like Model Cities are best accomplished in cities where there are parity patterns of resident influence, an arrangement under which citizens, planners, and political leaders work together. However, it also appears that this arrangement is most likely to come about in communities in which there are, to being with, high degrees of political integration and low-to-moderate degrees of conflict.

We suggested in chapter 4 that if one studies communities over time, it would not be unlikely to find that the generation of conflict is required to achieve higher degrees of political integration in communities whose subsegments are isolated and alienated from the larger political system. Thus, by itself, conflict and the high degrees of resident influence, and the resident organization autonomy that it may generate, are not necessarily undesirable. However, we do think that it is useful for planners and policy makers to understand the functions of conflict and resident organization autonomy. They may be useful in achieving social goals that, in a given community, are of greater importance than the planning objectives of a particular program. For example, they may *eventually* bring about new arrangements for community decision making. But the Model Cities evidence indicates that they do not facilitate program planning and implementation.

Given a choice, resident influence has a more positive impact on planning and implementation of a program when it is directed into an institutionalized system for community decision making. Extreme degrees of resident influence that take shape in autonomous organizations that challenge the institutionalized system of planning do not result in positive program outcomes. When planners are interested in increasing citizen participation in planning, and when there is sufficient flexibility in the system for them to be able to open up new alternatives for the community, they would be wiser to push for *increased citizen influence in the institutionalized structure of planning rather than for the development of separate and autonomous structures.*

Chief Executive

The chief executive's positive influence in the planning and implementation of the Model Cities Program is clear in respect to all outcomes. But it is most strongly evident in regard to the acquisition of both categorical and local funds for the CDP and in the spending of supplemental funds. These findings underscore the propositions discussed in chapter 2 as well as conventional planning wisdom, which link chief executive commitment to program implementation. Community planning ventures similar in nature to the Model Cities Program are unlikely to prosper without chief executive support. Needless to say, planners in such programs are well advised to cultivate the active support of local political leadership.

Role Behavior of Planners

The findings in this area lend themselves to alternative interpretations. On the one hand they offer tentative support to the utility of task- and process-oriented behaviors for the achievement of task and process objectives, respectively. On the other hand, it appears that when program development contains a mix of objectives, each of these orientations is better suited to a particular phase of development than the other. Specifically, the findings imply that *emphasis on process-oriented behavior may be more productive in the initial planning phase, and emphasis on task-oriented behavior more productive in the implementation phase of program devleopment.*

However, it is important that any interpretation of these findings be placed in context. Whether the findings can be generalized beyond the early experiences in the Model Cities Program is open to question because during the period of investigation the CDAs were new agencies that came to cities with a broad claim to do comprehensive social and physical planning. Many of the local groups and organizations whom the CDAs wanted to engage in planning were already involved in their own social and physical planning activities and had achieved some degree of consensus about which activities were in each of their domains prior to the CDAs' arrival. As they moved into these interorganizational fields, the CDAs threatened the existing domain consensus. Under these circumstances a process orientation in the initial planning phase may have been especially practical to soothe apprehensions and to mitigate the disruptive influence of the CDA. Rothman's observations on the implications of research about the planner's role orientation are relevant here:

> In assessing the proper extent of directive role performance, practitioners should take into account the situational context, goals being sought, and attitudes of community participants. . . . Target groups that are distrustful or that feel a sense of distance or inferiority with respect to the practitioner may react negatively to the exercise of more assertive roles; hence, the practitioner should be cautious in regard to assertiveness with such clients and constituencies until trust is established, or disparity in knowledge or skill is reduced.[1]

Hence, the generally favorable results of process-task phasing may have had to do more with the newness of the Model Cities Program and its unsettling effects on the environment than with any intrinsic utility of an initial emphasis on process-oriented behavior in program development. The question remains whether task-oriented directors might have achieved higher outcome ratings on task objectives in the planning phase under less turbulent and tense circumstances than those experienced during the early days of Model Cities. The answer awaits further investigation in other progammatic contexts.

In conclusion, we can sum up our impressions of the Model Cities Program as follows: it did not significantly reduce poverty in America; to have thought that it would was an egregious error. It did not reform the federal system of categorical grants; to have placed that expectation upon the program was unreasonable. However, the Model Cities Program did offer many useful services to those in need; at the same time it provided federal and local planners and policymakers opportunities to experiment with, and increase their understanding of the resources and political arrangements that would be needed to realize those larger ogjectives, thus contributing further insights into the dynamics of community planning.

NOTES

1. Jack Rothman, *Planning and Organizing for Social Change* (New York: Columbia University Press, 1977), p. 75.

Index

Abrams, Charles, 22
Aiken, Michael, 41, 42, 45, 130, 131, 134, 173
Alford, Robert R., 41, 42, 45, 90, 130, 131, 134, 173
Alonso, William, 22
Anderson, Clinton, 162
Anderson, Martin, 22
Anderson, Walter O., XVII
Arnstein, Sherry, 34, 43, 44, 91
Austin, David M., 40, 42, 43, 45, 129, 134

Banfield, Edward C., XXIII, XXV, 19, 22
Baskin, Jane, 62
Beasly, James, XVII
Bell, Andrew, XVII
Bellush, Jewel, 43, 134
Bennet, Eleanor C., XXIV
Bergunder, Ann F., XXV
Bibby, John, 22
Blau, Peter M., 87, 88, 92
Bloomberg, Warner, 139, 156
Bolan, Richard S., 44, 122, 123
Brager, George, 90, 91, 180
Brown, Charlane, XVIII
Butler, John, 43

Cartwright, Dorwin, 43, 123
Cavanaugh, Jerome, 6

Chu, Susan, XVIII
Churchman, C. West, 43
Clark, Kenneth B., 22, 43, 65, 90
Clark, Terry, 45
Clute, Peter, XVII
Cotton, John F., XXIII
Crain, Robert, 45

Davidoff, Paul, 44, 92
Davidson, Roger, 22
Davis, David W., XXV, 24, 90, 91
Davis, James A., 62
Dawson, Richard E., 91
Demuth, Christopher C., XXIV
Dentler, Robert, 4, 22, 43, 134, 141, 156
Dill, William, 36, 44
Dodge, Don, XVII
Dodge, Robert, XVII
Durkheim, Emile, 47, 62
Dye, Thomas, 40, 45

Eaton, Joseph, 139, 156
Egan, Conrad, XVII
Epstein, Irwin, XXIV, 92
Erber, Ernest, 44
Erhardt, Walter, XVII
Etzioni, Amitai, 44, 89, 92

Fellin, Phillip, XXIV
Fowler, Edmond P., 72, 91

Freeman, Linton C., 62
Frej, William, 24, 133, 134
Frieden, Bernard J., XXIV, XXI,
    XXV, 18, 22, 25, 171, 173
Friedmann, John, 62, 145, 156

Gans, XVII
Gilbert, Evan, III
Gilbert, Jesse, III
Gilbert, Neil, XVIII, XX, XXV, 22,
    23, 43, 44, 90, 91, 92, 134, 139,
    156, 157, 173, 181
Godschalk, David R., 22
Goodman, Leo, 62
Greer, Scott, 4, 22, 134
Grosser, Charles F., 139, 156
Gurin, Arnold, 44, 91, 92

Haar, Charles M., XXIV, XXV, 6
Haas, J. Eugene, 92
Hall, Richard, 92
Hare, A. Paul, 123
Hausknecht, Murray, 134
Hawkins, Brett W., 92
Heineman, Ben, 6
Hickson, D., 92
Hill, Ursula, XVII
Hinings, C.R., 92
Hollander, Theodore E., 33, 44
Hopkins, Jeanette, 22, 43, 90
Hopps, June G., XXIV
Hunter, Floyd, 44
Huntington, Samuel P., 156
Hyde, Floyd H., 24
Hyman, Herbert H., 43

Jacob, Herbert, 91
Jacobs, Jane, 69, 70, 90
James, Judson L., 7, 10, 15, 17, 23,
    24, 150, 156, 157, 162, 173
Janis, Michael, XVII
Johnson, David D., XVII
Johnson, Lyndon B., 2, 6, 10, 16, 17,
    22, 68
Johnson, Norman J., 92
Johnson, Sarah, XVIII
Jordan, Fred, XXV, 6, 7, 23, 24

Kahn, Alfred J., XVII, 22
Kaiser, Edgar, 7
Kaitz, Edward M., 43
Kaplan, Marshall, XVII, XXI, XXIV,
    XXV, 18, 22, 23, 24, 25, 173
Kennedy, John F., 2
Koory, Richard, XVII
Kramer, Ralph, 43, 44, 91
Kruskal, William, 62

Kuo, Wen H., 39, 44, 45

Lawson, Simpson, 23
Lee, Eugene C., 90, 91
Legates, Richard, 24
Levine, Jacob, 43
Levitan, Sar A., 22
Lieberman, Bennie, XVII
Lineberry, Robert L., 72, 91
Lindblom, Charles E., 156
Lindsay, John, 9
Lippitt, Ronald, 43, 134, 140, 156
Lubove, Roy, 22

Mangum, Garth L., 22
Mayer, Robert, 43
McBroom, Elizabeth, 92
McGaugh, Marcy, XVIII
McLean, John W., XVII
Merton, Robert K., 91, 92
Mogulof, Melvin, XXIII, 33, 43, 90,
    172, 173
Montagna, P., 92
Morris, Robert, 22
Moynihan, Daniel P., 22, 65, 90
Mumford, Lewis, 2
Muskin, Selma J., XXIII

Nathan, Richard, XXIII
Newman, Edward, XXIV
Nixon, Richard M., 16, 18, 19, 67,
    134, 172
Nutt, Thomas E., 22

O'Brien, Lawrence, 9
O'Donnel, Edward J., 22
O'Flaherty, Kevin, XXIV
Osborn, Michelle, 43
Ozawa, Martha N., XXIII

Parenti, Michael, 91
Paul, Benjamin, 92
Paulson, Robert, XVIII
Payne, Anna, XVII
Perlman, Robert, 44, 91, 92
Perloff, Harvey, XXIII
Pollack, David, XVII
Pollinger, Annette, 43
Pollinger, Kenneth, 43
Potter, Kinsey, XVII
Pugh, D.S., 92

Rabinovitz, Francine F., 22, 35, 36,
    38, 44, 144, 145, 156
Raegan, Michael D., XXIII
Rafsky, William, 6
Rains, Albert, 8

Reuther, Walter, 6
Ribicoff, Abraham, 6
Roberts, Lynne, XVIII
Robinson, James A., 91
Romney, George, 16, 17, 20, 25, 90
Rose, Steven M., XXV, 38, 43, 44
Rosencranz, Armin, XVII, 25, 92
Rosenstock, Florence, 139, 156
Rosenthal, Donald, 39, 45
Rossi, Peter H., XXIV, 4, 22, 43, 44, 134, 141, 156
Rothman, Jack, 43, 82, 83, 91, 92, 179, 180

Sanders, Irwin T., 91
Schmandt, Henry J., 156
Schon, Donald A., 22
Simpson, George, 62
Shostak, Arthur B., 43
Slotnik, Barbara, XVII
Sparkman, John, 8
Specht, Daniel, III
Specht, Eliot, III, XVIII
Specht, Harry, XVIII, XX, XXV, 24, 25, 44, 90, 91, 92, 133, 134, 181
Specht, Riva, XVIII
Spergel, Irwin, 92
Stein, Clarence, 2
Sullivan, Marilyn, 22
Sundquist, James L., XXV, 24, 90, 91
Sze, William C., XXIV

Taggart, Robert III, 22
Taylor, Ralph, 12, 23, 77, 78, 91

Terrell, Paul, XXIII
Thomas, Edwin J., XXIV, 91, 123
Thompson, James D., 37, 44
Tripodi, Tony, XXIV
Tuite, John, XVII
Turem, Jerry, XXIV
Turner, C., 92
Turner, John, 91

Van Til, Jon, 43
Van Til, Sally B., 43
Vines, Kenneth, 91

Walter, Claude L., XXIV
Warren, Roland L., XXIV, XXV, 15, 24, 34, 36, 37, 43, 44, 90, 91, 173
Weaver, Robert, 7, 9, 10, 13
Webber, Melvin, 22
Weisinger, Marvin, XXIV
Weiss, Carol H., XXIV
White, Ralph, 43
Wildavski, Aaron, 145, 156
Williams, Walter, XXIV
Willmann, John B., 161, 173
Wilson, James Q., 42, 43, 45, 134, 173
Wolfe, Tom, 90
Wolfinger, Raymond E., 91
Wood, Robert C., 6, 7, 13, 162

Yin, Robert K., 34, 36, 40, 42, 44, 90, 129, 134
Young, Whitney, Jr., 6

Zander, Alvin, 43, 123

About the Authors

Neil Gilbert, Professor at the School of Social Welfare, University of California, Berkeley, was director of the Research Division of Pittsburgh's Community Action Agency 1966 to 1968. His analysis of that program was presented in his book, *Clients or Constituents* (Jossey Bass, 1970). He has, in addition, done research on problems of race relations, social welfare, and social planning which is reported in several books, monographs, and articles published in such journals as *Social Work, Social Service Review, Society,* and *Public Administration Review.*

Harry Specht, Professor at the School of Social Welfare, University of California, Berkeley, directed community action programs in New York and California from 1960 to 1966. His work is reported in *Community Organizing* (with Brager, Columbia University Press, 1973). He has also done research on young adults, social planning, and social welfare that is reported in several books, monographs, and articles in such journals as *Children, Social Work,* and *Policy and Politics.*

Gilbert and Specht have collaborated on numerous works. Their joint publications include: *Dimensions of Social Welfare Policy* (Prentice-Hall, 1974), *The Emergence of Social Welfare and Social Work* (Peacock, 1976), and *Planning for Social Welfare* (Prentice-Hall, 1977). They began their study of the Model Cities Program in 1971 and have published several reports and papers on the subject. In this volume they report their findings in respect to the major purpose of the Model Cities study, which was to test propositions in community planning. Both authors teach social planning, social policy, and program evaluation.